MASTERS OF FLINT

MASTERS OF FLINT

by

A. J. FORREST

TERENCE DALTON LIMITED
LAVENHAM . SUFFOLK

1983

Published by
TERENCE DALTON LIMITED

ISBN 0 86138 015 0   Hardback
ISBN 0 86138 016 9   Limp covers

Text photoset in 11/12 pt. Baskerville

Printed in Great Britain at
The Lavenham Press Limited, Lavenham, Suffolk

Contents

Dedicated to the lady whose foot,
mistaking my head for a rung,
interrupted my descent to the
bottom of Grime's Graves.

Index of Illustrations

Acknowledgements

THIS work could not have been attempted far less completed without much generous assistance. Dr N. A. M. Rodger, Assistant Keeper at the Public Records Office, Kew, introduced me to the different classes of Board of Ordnance records. Mr G. de G. Sieveking, Deputy Keeper of the British Museum's Department of Prehistory and Romano-British Antiquities, helped to clarify my conception of Grime's Graves. Lord Energlyn, Professor of Geology at the University of Nottingham, 1949-78, gave me his views on the formation and properties of flint. Mr David Brown of the Department of Antiquities, the Ashmolean Museum, Oxford, allowed me to consult his study of pursemounts and firesteels. To Mr W. S. Curtis, of the Muzzle Loaders Association of Great Britain, I owe some insight into that organisation's activities, and he also provided me with historical material from his personal collection.

I received guidance on specific points from Mr Howard L. Blackmore, Deputy Master of the Armouries at the Tower of London, Professor J. K. S. St Joseph, of Selwyn College, Cambridge, Miss Elizabeth Owles and Mr Gavin Jenkins, curator and assistant curator respectively of Moyses Hall Museum, Bury St Edmunds, Miss Barbara Green, Keeper of Archaeology at the Castle Museum, Norwich, Mr Stephen Green, of the National Museum of Wales, Cardiff, Miss Fiona Marsden, curator of the Sussex Archaeological Society, Mr Peter Northeast, chairman of the Suffolk Local History Council, Mr Rex Whitta, head ranger of Thetford Chase, Mr W. L. Fox, of Long Melford, Suffolk, Mr B. D. Walsh, an authority on railway history, and Mr Barrie Jakeman, Agitant-Generalle of The Sealed Knot.

Mr Denys Parsons, of the British Library, Mr P. N. Allen, of the City of Birmingham's Reference Library, and Miss S. M. Arnold, of the Royal Institution's Library, also responded generously to my inquiries.

Much help came from overseas. Mr Steve L. Pistono, of Naperville, U.S.A., gave details of America's interest in flintlocks for sport and competitions; Mr David A. Armour, of Mackinac Island State Park Commission, Michigan, provided data on flints found at Fort Michilimackinac and elsewhere in North America; Mr John H. Grenville, Historical Research Officer of Old Fort Henry, Ontario, advised me about Canadian flintlock ceremonies; and Mr T. J. Shaughnessy, Manager of Old Fort Erie, told me of Brandon's role in its animation programme. I received valuable research advice from Mrs Elizabeth F. Hale, Librarian of the Society of the Montreal Military and Maritime Museum. Miss Elisabeth Mundgaard, of the Danish

National Museum, Copenhagen, supplied details of the Hindsgavl dagger, and Mr M. C. Quinnel and Mr R. Robins of Queensland Museum's Department of Anthropology and Archaeology forwarded copies of Sydney B. J. Skertchly's catalogue of his flints collected in Brandon and district, which he donated to their museum, and details of his thirty-year residence in South-east Queensland.

Close to home, I am particularly indebted to Mr Seymour de Lotbiniere for his encouragement and generosity in recounting his own researches. Mr James English, the owner of Brandon's surviving flint knapping business, also gave ready help, and likewise Mr Fred Avery, formerly a full-time knapper, but now engaged in the craft part-time. Mr Charles Killingworth, Mr Herbert Field, Mr and Mrs Albert Wing, Mr Albert Palmer, Mr Arthur Moreton and Canon John Fitch provided details I could not otherwise have obtained. I must declare a special debt also to the late Mr Herbert Edwards, who was for more than thirty years the industry's chief proprietor and mainstay.

I received much practical help and stimulus from Mr Peter Burrin. Nor would this work have reached a conclusion without the ever ready staff assistance and resources of the London Library, the Suffolk Record Office at Bury St Edmunds and the new Central Library at Norwich, the facade of which, appropriately, is panelled in Brandon-prepared flint.

To all my gratitude is very real, but on my head alone rests responsibility for any textual errors or omissions in acknowledgement.

Photographs

APART from government departments, musems and institutions named for supplying particular prints, I am most grateful for the loan of photographs to Mr James English, Mr Seymour de Lotbiniere, Mr Herbert Field and Mr and Mrs Albert Wing. Mr Brian Turner, chairman and founder of Lakenheath's Camera Club, supplied me with studies of Grime's Graves and Brandon town and inn signs. And Mr Terry Moore, a professional photographer, deserted his London beat to face the hazards of a journey into East Anglia and record for me notable examples of medieval flintwork.

A. J. FORREST

Brandon, Suffolk

CHAPTER ONE

A Locality of Haunting Timelessness

FLINT, though among the earliest materials handled by man, still challenges geologists to say exactly how it originated. During the Cretaceous Age, 135 to 65 million years ago ("creta" being Latin for chalk), a vast sea flowed partially over land masses attached to what we now identify as continents. This milky water, caused by lime-secreting organisms, covered tracts of Europe including the British Isles, a mere offshoot which broke away from the mainland only a few thousand years ago.

Those ponderous, jaw-snapping, predatory and incredibly ugly monsters, the Dinosauri, disappeared into the chalky sludge, bequeathing their skeletons to fossil beds along with all kinds of cretaceous plant and marine life.

Flint has a mosaic-like structure. Mineralogists describe it as micro or crypto-crystalline quartz, the greater percentage of which is silica derived from glassy sandstone grains. Over a 70-million-year time cycle, the particles drifting in the chalky sea aggregated. As the waters drained away during the Ice Ages' six or so glaciations and land levels rose, flint was formed in the chalk by chemical action. These secretions sometimes lie in horizontal courses between beds of chalk as flat, layered slabs, tabular flint, but more frequently they appear as nodules coated, like the slabs, by a hard white rind, the cortex. Their shapes take on an infinite variety. Sometimes the flint grains were precipitated in vertical pipes, hollow and cylindrical.

So, by infinitessimal gradations, there surfaced chalk-rich islands, of which the Isle of Wight is one and Britain less modestly another, with folds of wealds, downs and ridgeways marking the heaviest concentrations. Escarpments and hills, so endowed, attest their modern permanence by intriguing landmarks such as the White Cliffs of Dover, the White Horse of Uffington in Berkshire, the Long Man of Wilmington in Sussex, a chalk figure 226 feet tall that "looks naked towards the shires", or Dorset's rampant giant at Cerne Abbas, measuring 180 feet from head to toe, with a 30-foot phallus.

Of the three subsections of the Cretaceous Age, the Uper Chalk houses the main deposits of flint; it appears less stratified in the Middle and Lower Chalk, though it can and does occur anywhere in chalk formations. In chalky districts of India, geologists have discovered relatively young deposits of flint, aged much less than 90 million years. And just as the chalk masses or beds differ in

◀ Arthur "Trixie" Drewry knapping flints at Brandon in 1961.

weight and quality, even in colour, from region to region, because of their marine composition, so does the flint within them.

Its identity "prints" can now be registered. Scientists drill a tiny sample, a core of half a gram, out of a piece of flint or a flint artefact, say an axe-head, dissolve it in hydrofluoric acid, and by an analytical process known as atomic absorption spectrometry expose its mineral trace elements of aluminium, potassium, magnesium and sodium, and fractional clay content. By comparing results of combinations recorded with a regional flint map such as the British Museum is preparing, the archaeologist can determine from which district, sometimes even from which quarry, a flint artefact originated.

Flint, a hard opaque material only three shades softer than diamond and capable of scratching glass, is acid resistant and magnificently durable. It appears in a startling colour range, black, steely grey, bluish, pale violet, brown, amber or honey-coloured and white, but all lumps and nodules when fractured betray their seabed ancestry. They have no grain, but when hammer-struck break into conchoidal or wave-like shapes suggestive of a mussel-shell's back. On this characteristic the flint knapper* builds his craft. Flint, again, fractures sharply, yielding edges razor-like in keenness and translucent to the point of beauty when thin and newly chipped.

A chalk belt, rich in flint accretions, runs from East Yorkshire to North Norfolk, then sweeps on a broad front through and beyond East Anglia in a south-westerly direction, taking in as its width narrows St Albans and the Chilterns and running on through the Marlborough and the White Horse Downs and Salisbury on its way to Dorchester and South Devon. There is a good flint-bearing region in Hampshire around Winchester, and a generous belt seams the Sussex Downs. Chalk again yields its treasure in North-west Kent, and along the brows of the Thames Estuary.

As a primary field for flint, the Breckland of East Anglia can claim in its lower levels some of the finest black flint handled by man. It accounts for the eminence of Grime's Graves at Weeting, Norfolk, as the largest prehistoric flint mining site in Britain, and for the supremacy of the gunflint industry at Brandon on the Suffolk flank of the Little Ouse River, only two and a half miles distant. Flint, dug from different parts of these two counties, embellishes many of their finest medieval churches and ancient buildings.

Brandon as a small town is virtually unique in being built on flint foundations, natural and hammered. Today the people there who muster about 7,000 own no particular allegiance to this brittle, expressive stone. But, if not benefiting from it, their pride in the town's long-standing association with the world's oldest craft assumes intriguing and visible shapes, not simply roadways like Knappers Way or Rattlers Road. The Market Hill, overlooked by the asymmetrical clock tower of the Forest Heath Primary School, displays the town sign, a stylised tableau mounted on a pillar with a flint mottled base,

---

*Knap from the Dutch *knappen*—to crack.

The town sign on Market Hill, Brandon, with the *Flint Knappers* on the right and High Street in the background.   *Brian Turner*

in which one figure ladles out flints while his two partners set to work with their hammers.

A similar motif, but executed more realistically, adorns the wall panel above the entrance to the *Flint Knappers* standing on the hill's north-east corner at its junction with Thetford Road. In 1934, this pub superseded the old stone-built *Eagle*, for long a popular tavern in the town. As a mark of distinction for the new building, uniquely named, I believe, and a prelude also to increased trade, the artist, A. H. Thirtle, designed a copper plate representation of a flint knapper seated in his workshop manufacturing gunflints.

For those familiar with the craft his shop looks a trifle too clean and orderly. There is no hint of the enshrouding, suffocating, lung-destroying dust. A pendulum wall clock ticks away the minutes of a past age. Nodules and hammers lie on the floor. There is a knapping hammer with spare blades hanging on the back wall. Of baskets filled with gunflints or holding flakes ready for knapping, one shows a bottle neck, possibly concealing the craftsman's tipple. At night the panel is illuminated.

Quite apart from the population explosion, bringing Brandon's inhabitants to 4,545 at the 1971 census, modernisation has swept through the town almost like a tornado. London overspill, resulting in a GLC estate, paved the way for large-scale reconstruction and development schemes and introduced fresh blood into the town. The old part, west of St Peter's, the parish church, called Town Street, once resembled a Scottish fisher village with its flint cottages, two up and two down, yards and outside loos, and fiercely independent spirit. Bungalow estates have displaced this settlement and spread far beyond it. Yet for all the present-day hunger for change, some fine examples of flintwork remain, among them the row of cottages, built in 1883, where I write this study. Another is a house in Lode Street, easily identifiable by a stone lion guarding its portal, whose north wall of black flint squares set in lime mortar has weathered 130 winters or more and, if appearances count, looks fit to last for centuries more.

Conservationists decry the disappearance of flint dwellings, in some places the obliteration of whole streets, whose walls have been crushed as solid

The copper plate panel above the entrance to the *Flint Knappers* at Brandon.

Brian Turner

foundation for new buildings, shops, offices, toilets and car parks. Happily Brandon's family links with flint are not so easily torn asunder or pushed underground. There remains a healthy muster of people with names evocative of flint knapping mastery such as Snare, Field, Edwards, Palmer, Carter, Basham, Waterman, Wharf, Jacob, Ashley and Dyer. The craft of knapping itself survives. True, it has lost much of its impetus, but periodically demands for its skills arise, at times from unexpected quarters.

What of Brandon's inheritance? For more than a hundred years gunflints manufactured in the town crossed most of the world's frontiers. From a national viewpoint, their finest hour occurred at Waterloo when they struck fire in the muskets of Wellington's "unbroken squares". Admittedly Wellington and his Prussian ally, Blücher, lost 30,000 men, and it was, as the Duke avowed, "a damned serious business . . . the nearest run thing you ever saw in your life". But in vain did the Old Guard charge recklessly against his disciplined troops, to be mown down by hails of bullets released by sparks from the dark flints cocked in their muskets.

If soldiers handled their flintlocks more confidently when these were fitted with Brandon's black gunflints, so did tribal hunters in various regions and different hemispheres. In some territories, flints, though ostensibly knapped for firearms, never saw the flash of priming powder, being passed from hand to hand as objects of barter, even tribal currency.

Though a harsh sequel to a manufacturer's aims, but one to which we have become accustomed in modern wars, bullets or ball discharged by sparks from flint-struck steel at times killed or injured compatriots of those who made the gunflints. Settlers in New Zealand during the Maori Wars, for example, came under fire from muskets and carbines so flinted.

If factors of distance and time could be related, instead of posing a ratio of insoluble complexity, because the required mathematical data can never be deduced, it would be intriguing to draw up a balance sheet between miles and years. For granted that Brandon gunflints have journeyed hundreds of thousands of miles, igniting guns from Greenland's icy mountains to India's coral strand and beyond, just how far has the mileage clocked up in any particular year overshadowed the millions of years required by these flint exports to surface from their birthplace?

A guardian spirit, I have long maintained, presides over that birthplace. Through its presence, the locality surrounding Brandon enjoys some immunity from contemporary frets and has an inbuilt reservoir of strength to withstand such disturbances as the menacing roar of American supersonic swing wing F-111's hurtling across its skies. Its power is embedded deep in Breckland. It is a natural shock absorber. Julian Tennyson in his *Suffolk Scene* (1939) noted this special quality when he saw buses coasting along a nearby road, and from where he stood on a Breckland heath heard no sound of their passing.

Grime's Graves in 1980, with the mouths of infilled pits and, at left, the Department of the Environment's exhibition centre.   *Brian Turner*

The landscape has undergone radical changes since the Forestry Commission put down its roots in 1922. Now the Commission manages about 50,000 acres of Breckland, stretching from Swaffham in the north to Culford in the south, from Harling in the east to Mildenhall in the west. About ninety per cent of its plantations are coniferous, each one systematically planted and felled. The now-thriving green umbrella obliterates all traces of what were formerly warrens swarming with rabbits, sandy and scrubby wastes, sporting estates, and semi-destitute farms, haunts of lark and curlew.

Chemically, chalk consists of carbonate of lime with some impurities; it is usually white or creamy coloured, but can be stained a pale yellow or a pallid green. That forming Breckland's backbone is remarkable for its thickness, belts of rocklike solidity bonded inside it. In Norfolk, chalk descends to a greater depth than elsewhere in Britain, and nodules of black flint as well as tabular slabs, with which it is layered like fillings in a sandwich, are of a rich texture, little fossil ridden, and knap sound. Embedded from ten to fifty feet below the topsoil, they constitute the very substance of man's slow emergence from animalism.

Four thousand years ago at Grime's Graves, north-east of Brandon, Neolithic tribespeople mined this flint by techniques more sophisticated than primitive. The Graves, dented by shaft infillings, cover 93 acres. No larger or more famous flint mining complex exists in Britain.

There, within the official site's boundaries, much smaller than its full extent, the locality's haunting timelessness almost stills the air. This atmosphere, calm, reassuring and magical, came close to overwhelming me before Easter Sunday, 1963, when I kept a night's vigil at the Graves. As I tramped in semi-darkness from my flint cottage, I felt as if seeking a rendezvous with man's destiny. Arrived at Grime's Graves, I threaded my way, slow in step but quick in imagery, along the paths twisting in and out among the silver birches and hawthorn clumps overhanging the grassy, cup shaped hollows, the long silent mouths of ancient man's pits. It was easy to visualise those who once sweated inside this hill, fighting the unknown as they dug shafts and tunnelled galleries underfoot. Hypnotised by fancy, I half expected their ghosts to steal out of the knoll, rush up gesticulating excitedly and, if not hostile, display their flint hauls, stone hammers, tools and weapons, and perhaps escort me inside a pit. As one stares at a bush in half light, so it appears to move, and heaps of white chalk exposed here and there aligned with the dappled silver boles of birches simulated a phantom atmosphere.

Soon it poured with rain. The fast descending water curtain accentuated the night's silence, interrupted only by owls hooting from distant trees. Red stags, roe deer, red squirrels and other Breckland creatures, if bedded down, had better shelter than I found pressing my back against an eave-topped wall of the custodian's hut. But despite pelting rain, my absorption deepened into a kind of mystical communion with a Stone Age flintfield, still vibrant, its influence pervasive and seemingly permanent.

Was I not standing on a matriarchal womb of human craftsmanship? From those pits man's desire for mastery over his material world had acquired meaning and impetus. The flint he extracted drew out his skills. Today, he expresses his craft by high technology, his ability to walk on the moon, his nuclear resources, power stations, satellite communications, sputniks and space probes, as well as his stocks of deadly bombs, potential destroyers of his species. Unless he had first mastered flint, such achievements and such nightmares might still be beyond his compass.

On a more active front, I campaigned hard that year to prevent the Ministry of Works, the then responsible department, from cutting down the silver birches and other trees growing beside the pits, not simply because they harboured on Easter morning a triumphant dawn chorus of bird song, an immense reinvigoration after a drenching night. But letters of protest given prominence in the *Eastern Daily Press* (Norwich), *East Anglian Daily Times* (Ipswich) and *Bury Free Press* (Bury St Edmunds) as well as appeals to the Ministry and the Council for the Preservation of Rural England brought no joy. The Ministry, forgetful of the site's shady setting in earlier times, held that trees and shrubs endangered the pit depressions, spoiling their shapes by root growth. The Forestry Commission knew better and offered to trim back the trees. They were not spared.

Whoever took this decision was soon confounded. Not only did the site lose its aesthetic appeal through the sacrifice of sentinel birches but their removal proved a nonsense from a conservationist's viewpoint. It led to unrestricted growth of saplings. A fresh clearance took place during the winter of 1979/80. The pits were cleaned of undergrowth, bushes cut down to ground or stump level and, as some insurance for the future, the site was let to a farmer for sheep grazing to restrict sapling growth. At present, the Graves wear a stripped, denuded look as bare as newly shorn ewes.

To discover what might befall, in May, 1963, I invited Mr William Youngs, of Harleston, Norfolk, a dowser since 1927 and a life member of the British Society of Dowsers, to give his whalebone rod a run over Grime's Graves. He opted for whalebone as it was stronger than the traditional hazel twig and less inclined to blister his hands. While we walked over ground not marked by any surface dents or hollows, his rod twisted madly, a sign, he said, of tunnels below. In pit No. 15, then open for public viewing, he tested the shaft's floor from which eight galleries diverged; again his rod twisted vigorously like a living thing. It indicated, he said, a cavity twelve feet or so below this level. Did the Neolithic miners dig even deeper than the black flint seam, expecting to find more of it, richer material or a water channel?

Summing up Mr Young's exploration in an *East Anglian Daily Times* article, printed 9th August, 1963, I wrote: "There are more galleries radiating from the central or main pits of Grime's Graves and spread over a wider area than can be suspected from any surface depression or markings." A great deal more than confirmation of the dowser's findings emerged in the 1970's when the British Museum's investigators examined the site and its surroundings.

Apart from their physical proximity, the relationship between Brandon and Grime's Graves tempts speculation. As that scholar and antiquarian with a genius for chilling ghost stories, Dr M. R. James, wryly remarked in his *Norfolk and Suffolk* (1930), "Brandon is famous for the flint knapping still carried on there, and probably there only, and (perhaps fondly) imagined never to have been disused since the days of flint implements."

A Report Slip for Suffolk Industrial Archaeology dated February, 1968, casts caution aside. It states categorically: "Brandon has the oldest industrial tradition in Great Britain, dating back to the making of flint weapons and tools at Grime's Graves for barter circa 2000 BC. The strike-a-light was the continuing tool from the Neolithic era to the First World War, when they were in demand owing to the match scarcity. The shaping of a flasher, strike-a-light or gunflint required the same technique."

To move away from speculation. Herbert Edwards, flint master, was the first man in the world to knap into a BBC microphone. He was landlord of the *Flint Knappers* when I first knew him. His father, Frederick Edwards, modelled for the figure depicted on the pub's illuminated panel. As an eight-year-old, young Herbert started to learn the trade. As soon as he finished his midday meal, his father sat him before a block and taught him to knap. When the school bell rang for the afternoon session, he scampered back to his class. Three years later, his "homework" included evening stints under Fred Snare's instruction. This master knapper, who was most versatile in his craft, had a musical ear, and encouraged his apprentices to sing. While they perched on their knapping stools, young Edwards among them, he picked up his hammers and in the manner of a xylophone player beat out his favourite hymn tunes on flints of varying size and thickness. All in his workshop choir joined in the choruses, singing or belting out the words. He required competence of each boy as a knapper before allowing him to touch a quartering or flaking hammer.

A three-stage cycle governs the craft. First the quarterer, using a hammer about 3 lb in weight, picks up a nodule from a heap of raw flint freshly mined from Breckland's best seam. He balances it against a pad strapped to his left thigh and taps it lightly to sense its weak points. Then, knowing how to break it, he relies more on the hammer's weight than brute force to crack the nodule into workable pieces, "quarters". Ideally, one side of a "quarter" should be flat and smooth to give the desired flaking surface.

Robert Field (1869-1915) flaking, the most skilled process.
Herbert Field collection

Good flakers are rare. For the flaker's craft demands a refinement of strike, almost a jeweller's sensitivity to a mineral's breaking quality, implying the experience and confidence to fracture it adroitly. An inherited flint sense has a role here. Outsiders seldom attain the highest expertise.

Like the quarterer, the flaker first holds the "quarter" against his thigh pad and with a lighter but pointed hammer of soft steel strikes it so precisely that flakes, "double backs" or "single backs", i.e. ridged or ribbed with equidistant flanges, peel off the full length of his quarter, each of a width appropriate for cutting crosswise into gunflints.

The charm of flint from a craft standpoint stems from its myriad mosaics. Lacking grain like wood, it can be cut in any direction. Every hammer blow, too, results in a "bulb of percussion", a little swelling or bruise at the point where percussion occurred. Its appearance signifies an artificial fracture, the hallmark of man. It is illuminating to watch an experienced flaker stripping a "quarter" to its core. Each sharp blow from his hammer strikes the flint at an angle consistent with its weight, physical force used, wear of the hammer's point, volume of the quarter, length and even shape of flake. Fractures stream off, his padded leg acting as a springboard instead of a dead or solid base so that flint obeys its nature and falls away in conchoidal, slightly bulbous flakes.

Frederick Edwards, flint master, quartering and his young son Herbert knapping before the First World War. *James English collection*

The cycle is completed by the knapper who, seated at his block, a converted tree stump or portable table, has in front of him a buttressed iron stake projecting about three inches above the block's surface. He poises a flake, its flat face held upwards, against the iron's head. Then his lightweight hammer rises and falls as he strikes off a flint and trims it, first one side, then the reverse (my final chapter details the operation).

Herbert Edwards died in 1973, aged 81. The flint knapping industry, though not his first love, was assuredly his last and greatest. I had many conversations with him. Such exchanges were the easier because my cottage was not more than 200 yards from his flintworks and about the same distance from his home. And on several occasions I took notes of what he said.

When he left school at thirteen, his father set him to work in his flint shop behind the *Eagle*, but young Herbert soon began to chafe against knapping all day. His father, stricter than Fred Snare, kept him nose to flintstone. "After I'd had a turn in the workshop, he'd pick up different sets of flints I'd knapped and examine them carefully. If they weren't exactly right, he'd say, 'you must do better than this; put your mind to your work.' "

Discontent rose to a pitch. Bored by the monotony of knapping all day, or exasperated by his father's criticism, he dropped his knapping hammer and walked out. It speaks well for his parents' forebearance that they let him stay at home. To earn a shilling or two, he went rookscaring on a farm at Northcourt, west of Brandon. This refreshing open-air exercise lasted but a week or two. He then had a full-time job at William Rought's rabbit skin felting factory in George Street. Altogether his truancy from the family craft lasted five months. After that he reappeared in his father's knapping shop and settled down, a rebel no longer, with six or seven others in a hot dusty atmosphere where raucous coughs punctuated at times the persistent tinkle, clink and rattle of falling flints.

"We sat so close together," he said, "that several of us could shake hands without getting up. The older men hated draughts. They stopped up all cracks and blanketed the roof with sacking. If you touched it clouds of dust sifted down. There was plenty of it around, anyway, covering walls, windows and sills. In winter, we kept a good fire going; those nearest it sweated but didn't seem to mind."

Lack of fresh air showed in the men's dust-ingrained faces. The job taxed their hardihood, the more so when they worked ten to twelve hours a day. Health worsened. Stepping out of a frowsty workshop into wintry air, freezing or not, a knapper might curse his bronchial chest. Some died early of tuberculosis, others of pneumonia.

By completing his seven-year apprenticeship, young Edwards gained proficiency in each process of the gunflint craft from quartering to knapping, though he never perhaps felt completely at home flaking. His wages fitted the earnings structure of his day, but as the boss's son he picked up an extra shilling or two. "When I could turn out 2,000 gunflints in a day and earn 3s. 6d. (17½p.) an hour, I got married," he said. "Merchants then supplying the African trade paid us pre-1914-18 War 15s. (75p.) to £1 a thousand for best gunflints."

This remark touched off a folk memory of the industry's heyday when, during the Napoleonic wars, some Brandon knappers pocketed ten sovereigns in a week.

"Not a full week either. Many of these men were highly religious. They attended Sunday services smartly turned out and wearing top hats. What I

The restful dignity of a flint cottage.
James English collection

want to tell you is this; they worked only a four-day week, giving themselves full weekends, with Mondays off, long before citymen in London relaxed like that. But it wasn't a soft life. When they did work, from Tuesdays to Fridays, they started, in many instances, at 5 a.m. and did not knock off until 9 p.m.

"In my early days, one knapper, 'Champ' Palmer, kept traditional hours. As for the killing dust, which led to silicosis, when I was a youngster, no one thought about trying to control it. We just lived with it, and men died of it in their thirties or early forties."

Of celebrated knappers known to him as a boy, William "Billy" Carter was outstanding. "His flaking was absolutely perfect. He was so wrapped up with knapping that he made models of greyhounds out of flint. Father employed two men who were also exceptionally clever, 'Hebda' Field and Herbert 'Piper' Field. Everyone in the craft had a nickname. These were so widely used that we often forgot, and some of us never knew, their proper Christian names."

CHAPTER TWO

Bubberhutching on the Sosh

THE quiet stretch of field and plantations a mile and a quarter south-east of Brandon, Lingheath Farm, conceals more than a hundred years of flint mining activity. Its surface was once riddled with shafts sunk by lone miners, each dug laboriously with spade and single-pronged pick and banked by chalk and stone debris. Having hauled out all procurable black flint, miners sometimes partially filled in their pit openings or blocked them up with brushwood, but more often abandoned them, unstopped, for each crescent shaped crater to add a fresh scar to a barren perforated wasteland.

Outlines so engineered furrow the south wall towards the east end of the huge chalk pit quarried by the Brandon Lime Company at Taplins, just off the Thetford Road. These cavities in the chalk face descend to a flint seam about twelve feet below ground level. The line of nodules that escaped the miners' burrowings stands out sharply. In contemplating it, one's gaze travels back 65 to 90 million years.

Again, a short distance beyond the farm's eastern boundary, five or six pits lie open in Forestry Commission woodlands, one with its mouth nearly choked by a beech. In glimmering light an atmosphere of menace lurks by these gaping holes despite sheltering trees, carpets of green or russet bracken and the Commission's sensible precaution of screening off each shaft with wire netting. A stranger might fancy he had stumbled on lairs burrowed and then deserted by some fearsome prehistoric beast.

Short of having concrete poured in, the pits could not be filled up from head to base as they were always constructed in stages, in a series of descending platforms with toe holds cut in their chalk walls. Some, hidden beneath newly reclaimed fields, refuse to lie dormant but reappear with a thud or a bump, especially after heavy rains, as top fillings cave in under the weight of a tractor plough, a trailer loaded with sugar beet or a combine harvester.

Lingheath Farm occupies 183 acres. By an Enclosure Award of 15th February, 1810, the ground on which it lies was designated the "Poor's Allotment", but no free-for-all. A charity, the Lingheath Trust, managed the ground and administered its income for the benefit of Brandon's needy parishioners. In Victorian times and earlier, those "up against it" might view this grant as some consolation, though scarcely a generous one, for the parish's loss of common rights.

Although no flint is mined at Lingheath now, the farm retains an interest for Brandonians, a hundred or two of whom receive a Christmas bonus from the Trust's funds. From the outset the land yielded three sources of income; rents from leases of agricultural rights, rents from leases of sporting rights, and the royalties or groundage paid on flint extracted from it. On the agricultural side, such rentals kept step with farming values placed on Breckland's more impoverished or sandy, scrubby, rabbit-nibbled holdings. In 1819 the Trustees of the Poor's Allotment rented 12½ acres of heath to George Ashman, yeoman, for seven years at an annual rent of £5, his lease running until Michaelmas, 1826. For a similar term, 25 acres were let to John Utting, innkeeper, for £9 7s. 6d. a year; and John Snare, gunflint maker, also rented 25 acres for £10 a year, for the same term. In some years the heath's value below ground exceeded that on top.

A "local difficulty" occurred in 1822 when the Trustees, anxious to maximise their income to supplement parish relief, proposed to lease the heath's shooting rights. News of their intention drew a sharp reproof from the legal representatives of a Mr Bliss who, as Lord of the Manor, claimed "rights of free warren." It seemed to him outrageous that any organisation should consider letting "rights of sport" in the middle of a gentleman's estate. True, the holder of those rights might put down corn, hay or other bait to draw pheasants or deer away from adjoining land. But Mr Bliss, whatever his legal entitlement, deserves few plaudits because of his high-handed manner in associating his manorial rights with ownership of the flints lying under the ground and contending that it was only his "regard for the poor" that permitted other interests to exploit them. As Lord of the Manor for barely nine months, he might have familiarised himself with local feeling before rushing off in a huff to his solicitors at Bream's Buildings in Chancery Lane, London, and instructing them to draft and dispatch a churlish note.

Levies imposed by the Trustees inevitably drew complaints about their severity both from farming tenants and from purchasers of flints mined from the heath. In his supplement to *The Suffolk Traveller* (1844) Augustine Page said the agricultural rental was worth £16 a year, adding: "There is a flint quarry on the land which is let at a ground rent of 5s. for every load of flint taken from it."

While stone diggers continued their burrowings, the little land available for farming exasperated and, except for the rabbit crop, nearly starved those trying to earn a living from it. By 1885, the agricultural rental was £42 a year. Miners sinking shafts on a scheduled part of the heath did so at their own expense, and whoever bought the flint and chalk raised by their toils paid a groundage of 3d. (1p.) for each cartload of chalk removed and from 1s. (5p.) to 1s. 8d. (8p.) according to quality, for each cartload of flint.

At this period the capital administered by Lingheath's Trustees stood at

£2,054. This yielded an annual income of £113 18s. 2d. which, split up in equal portions, enabled 236 parishioners to receive sacks of coal for Christmas. The rules stipulated that each beneficiary must be head of a family, a legal settler, and in need. By 1891, the fund's balance was £2,436 7s. 8d. However, Lingheath Farm was leased to William Rought for £55. He also paid £30 for the groundage of flint and chalk withdrawals. These returns increased the sum available for distribution to £157 15s. 6d., out of which no fewer than 359 legal settlers had an issue of coal.

Until recent times, the Trustees confined their charitable awards to coal, based their allotment on a means test and restricted beneficiaries to those with not less than a three-year residential qualification in Brandon. But as new fuels such as gas, oil and electricity ousted ancient grates, and housing estates with centrally heated bungalows mushroomed over former woodland and farmland, coal lost its priority. Vouchers for fuel were then distributed; and in 1979 the Trustees handed out vouchers worth £3 for exchange by local shopkeepers either for fuel or food, and 189 applicants, all in fact who applied, received a voucher.

The Trustees also manage a far older fund, the Edmund Atmere charity of 1579, the proceeds of which devolved equally on the parishes of Foulden, Feltwell, Northwold and Weeting in Norfolk and Brandon in Suffolk. Atmere, thought to have been an Elizabethan shepherd, left about twenty acres of land at Old Buckenham for the benefit of those five parishes. Until recently his legacy brought meagre returns, since at times the rental from his land hardly met the expense of safeguarding it against flooding. When the Charity Commissioners, not surprisingly, agreed to its sale it hit a booming market, realising nearly five times the reserve placed on it.

Lingheath Farm in February, 1980, with a reclaimed field in the foreground. The scatter of flints and chalks conceals more than a hundred years of mining activity.

Mr and Mrs Charles Killingworth beside a caved-in flint shaft. This pit, long filled in, subsided in December, 1979, within fifty yards of their farmhouse.

Despite this windfall, Lingheath Farm as the territorial residue of the Poor's Allotment of 1810 remains the Trust's primary asset. As Mr Arthur Moreton, its chairman in 1980, told me: "We have to strike a nice balance between the interests of Brandon people and those of our farmer tenant. The Trust is bound to maintain the farm's fixtures, such as the farmhouse and barn, in working order, and although as Trustees we are under no statutory obligation to spend money on improvements other than those of a repair kind covenanted by the tenancy agreement, any extension or addition to the property should in the long term increase its value as an asset for Brandon."

In the 1950's a USAF plane crashed into the roadway leading to the farmhouse. Compensation for damage paid by the American authorities helped to fill more than one hole.

Before the 1939-45 war, a breeder of silver foxes hired the farm, built tall wire fences to confine his stock and erected an observation tower from which to watch their matings. But on the outbreak of war he joined the RAF. His foxes were pelted. Almost the sole survival of his enterprise consists of feeding bowls once used by his foxes but converted by one or two Brandon housewives into casserole dishes.

After occupation by the War Agricultural Committee, during whose tenure additional land was levelled and cultivated, the farm was let in 1948 to Mr Charles Killingworth, who is still the tenant today. Rent, always a contentious subject, raised certain difficulties. At one time a clerical trustee felt the farm was being leased at a rent less than a council house tenant was paying for his home. But with land values rocketing, absurdly to outsiders, the farm's rental, shooting rights included, jumped from £150 in 1962 to £600 in 1974 and £1,200 in 1980. Mr Killingworth's industry, his farming skills and eye for expansion partly account for these increases.

Most farmers, even of the toughest Scots-East Anglian breed, would surely have hurried back to their cars as soon as they saw his prospects in the 1940's. Where else in the county was there such a tortured lunar-like landscape, heavily cratered and pock-marked, its every aspect infertile, grim and forbidding? Now all is flat, green with fresh growth, and orderly.

"On arrival here," Mr Killingworth said, "we had just 44 acres fit for cultivation. The rest of the farm looked a wilderness of stones, chalk, trees and moss. It was overrun by rabbits. Scores of pits, each with heaps of stone and chalk round it, broke up the surface, tangled in parts by trees and scrub. You had to watch your step as you clambered around.

"We began with poultry, then turned to sheep, but neither venture brought much success. We lost several sheep because of falling into holes left by the miners. Struggling to get back on top, the sheep pitched over, and got stuck on their backsides, legs in air. Once turned over like that, they soon die if not righted."

By stubborn determination and a refusal to throw in his hand, however scrappy his crops, he and his two sons have brought 75 new acres under cultivation. "We bulldozed the piles of chalk and stone, first pulling out trees and bushes, to flatten the ground. Since then we've mucked it well. Pigs help here. But in spite of all, pits open up and every so often a machine's wheel drops into a hole as the ground gives way."

Not more than fifty yards from the farmhouse he showed me a circular hole, the top covering of a defunct shaft that had suddenly caved in a month earlier, in December, 1979. Again, at plough in March, 1980, his tractor was stopped midfield as another shaft opened up. Attached by a rope, he descended its first two stages and found the chalk walls as solid as if cut out yesterday.

His fields, when viewed in winter, look as if seeded with flints and chalk. Year after year, Mrs Killingworth picked stones off the land, ton by ton, until she hardly dare look at what still shows.

"In wet weather," he said, "the fields are unworkable. The chalk turns milky; it isn't surface chalk but stuff that has been carried up from below." He grows mainly barley and sugar beet and keeps a herd of pigs. Muck from their sties adds nutriment to the stone-speckled land, and helps him to wrest a livelihood from its thin, treacherous topsoil.

As Norfolk farmers say, "You've got to buy your land", meaning win if not woo it by sweat and persistence. That maxim fits him well, battling each season against rock and stone. But ironically, with a charity owning the property, it cannot be bought.

An ancient flint cottage formed part of the farmhouse when the Killingworths moved in. Its chimney, until dismantled, had a large open fireplace and was built of chalk blocks. The well on which the household relies

17

for water retains all its vintage purity; it is 135 feet deep, and except for some brickwork protecting the top drops sheer through chalk to water level. The entire farmstead, compared with those in the lush heavy clay districts of mid-Suffolk, has an air of wildness, of courageous improvisation; it is a pioneer settlement.

Nevertheless, beneath its tilth lies pioneering of a kind beside which the Killingworth family's tough labours must seem like preparations for a Christmas party.

As Herbert Edwards recalled: "My father in the 1900's employed four miners on Lingheath, Arthur 'Pony' Ashley, his brother Fred, known as 'Fretch', Jack Dyer and his son, Frank. Father paid each man piecework rates. No miner, and not many knappers at that time, had daywork wages."

All freshly mined flint, of whatever quality, was measured by the jag, normally about 13 cwt, but running sometimes to a ton. Edwards never heard of it being weighed. The flint masters measured it largely by eye.

"My father's method," he said, "was this. In bringing up flint from their pits, the miners piled it in heaps to make jags. As a check father, a tall man—he stood six feet—placed his toes together at the edge of a heap. He then stretched forward but without exerting himself pushed his walking stick into the ground on the opposite side, his body and stick forming an arch. If the space beneath seemed reasonably filled, he regarded the heap as a jag, and paid his stone digger the agreed price."

Working a good stratum of flint, a miner expected to raise from three to three and a half jags in a six-day week. As at Grime's Graves, three recognised seams lie embedded in the chalk under the heath, each separated by several million years of sedimentary action. The first met with in shaft sinking, "topstone", on the highest contour of the heath is found about 25 feet down and supplies poor quality flint, useful as foundations for buildings, roads or railway tracks. The second seam, "wallstone", a greyish flint, provides material mainly for wall facings. But what Lingheath and Neolithic miners alike coveted and scrabbled for is the third seam, "floorstone". It lies from forty to fifty feet down (much shallower down the ridge towards Santon Downham) and yields nodules and slabs of silky black, largely fossil-free flint, about the finest material Stone Age or Modern Age fabricators can shape.

The Lingheath Trust collected a royalty or groundage fee for every load of flint carted off the heath, unless all such rights for a particular year were leased. "These royalties," Herbert Edwards said, "never varied in my sixty years' experience. We always paid 10d. (4p.) a jag for 'topstone', 1s. 8d. (8p.) a jag for 'wallstone' and 3s. (15p.) a jag for 'floorstone'."

However exhaustively these stone diggers toiled they could not earn good money in return for long lonely stints which they spent burrowing underground with pick, hammer and shovel, hacking a man-sized hole through

A Lingheath miner stands in his pit mouth, surrounded by flint and chalk excavated from the shaft.   *Herbert Field collection*

chalk, much of it rock solid, to undermine nodules of white-skinned black flint. For some this mole-like existence persisted for years, indeed throughout a working life.

Rates paid for their excavations conformed to nearly the same uncompromising stability as royalties paid by flint masters to the Trust. As a rule a miner earned 2s. 3d. (11p.) a jag for "floorstone". In 1935 when in his seventies, "Pony" Ashley, a tall man of exceptional stamina and vigour even in old age, said his earnings seldom exceeded 12s. (60p.) a week. If he struck a good vein, he might raise an extra half jag to give his earnings a respectable look. He started stone digging when 12 years old and kept at it, in all weathers and seasons, without an appreciable break for sixty years.

"Miners, like knappers," said Herbert Edwards, "had their own customs as well as language. I never knew one to carry a watch. Setting off each day from their Brandon cottages with their 'dockey bags' (food carriers) they took two candles with them. Most men would be digging out flints by eight o'clock, often earlier, for each valued his independence. Descending his shaft, he lit his first candle. When it was half burnt out, he came up for a swig of tea, and when that candle expired, knew it was time for his 'dockey' (midday meal).

19

This might last thirty minutes or so. Then back to his burrow, where he lit his second candle and mined away until that died on him. Then he packed up for the day.

"Once a peculiar thing happened. It was a winter's night and seven o'clock had gone, and no sign of 'Pony' Ashley, Worried, and fearing an accident, his daughter called at the police station. The constable reassured her, telling her to go back home as he might already be there. He wasn't. More time passed and her worries grew. After she'd called again at the police station, the constable went with her to Lingheath, and there, much to their surprise, they found her father still working away at the bottom of his shaft. He had no idea of how late it was. Apparently he'd lit an extra candle and forgotten he'd done so."

Despite their preference for working alone without tackle or mechanical aid, Lingheath's miners rarely got into difficulties. Their lives depended on the solidity of the chalk in which they tunnelled, and on their instinct for gauging its rigidity without the use of pit props or artificial aids. Roof falls were exceptional. Nor mercifully did noxious gases, inflammable or poisonous, foul the burrows carved out on "gain", a term indicating horizontal direction as opposed to "fleet", their expression for depth. Occasionally loose sand or crumbly chalk tumbled down a shaft after breaking away from ground above the hard chalk levels. In thunderstorms, this silt might cascade or trickle through the different stages, and accumulate at the pit's toe. But such deposits were no more than a temporary inconvenience.

Arthur "Pony" Ashley, Lingheath's last full-time stone digger, standing among the mounds of excavated chalk and flint. *Sussex Archaeological Society*

The mining technique was clear-cut. Herbert Edwards explained it in detail during a conversation in March, 1962. "Start with an unbroken bit of heath. I could do it now or get a labourer to do it for me, after first paying a registration fee of 1s. 6d. to the clerk of Lingheath Trust. Arrived there with your tools, a pick, hammer and spade, you make your first cut, twelve feet by six feet. You then dig the soil out to the depth of your first staging, four foot six inches to five feet down. Most stagings are about that depth. Once there you cut out the centre, leaving a solid platform on three sides of the staging, and down you go, switching direction to the next level and so on stage by stage, each at right angles to the previous one, until you strike 'floorstone'."

This traditional system of sinking pits in stages, slantwise, gave rise to the phrase "bubberhutching on the sosh".* Romanticists detect a guttural sound in it, such as might have characterised, they suppose, the speech of Neolithic tribes. Last century, after this expression had surfaced from Lingheath's pits, it gained a circulation disconnected with stone digging. Brandon people applied it to anyone who, the worse for drink, could not walk upright or straight. Zig-zagging revellers may still be described as being "on the sosh", but the qualifying "bubberhutching" is no longer heard.

To follow Herbert Edwards underground. "Once he gets to the shaft's toe, 'floorstone' level, the miner works his way along the seam of black flint. He burrows in straight lines, his directions so far as he could estimate north, south, east and west. Each burrow runs ten to twelve yards in 'gain' from the toe, its height from two foot six to three feet, and width at the bottom three to four feet. That's kept flat, the rest of the burrow rounded."

What Edwards did not mention but later investigations made clear was the miner's habit of undermining his flint. He liked to look it in the face and pick underneath the seam to detach it.

Apses were cut at intervals to secure maximum yields from a burrow. Like his prehistoric forerunners at Grime's Graves, the miner lay for the most part on his side and picked away at the chalk while cramped or constricted. There was little space for swinging strokes, even with a one-pronged pick.

The picture emerges of a man battering away by candlelight in a narrow passage unseen by the world, divorced from its cheerful, sustaining sounds, the songs of birds and human voices, and with no one to talk to except the immobile and obdurate flints dumbly confronting him. Who is this creature disturbing their peace, fixed back in cretaceous time?

As he hacks away at the chalk rock to detach a nodule held vice-like in its grip, his exasperation suddenly interrupts the interminable tap, tap tap of his pick's point. "I'll have you, you bugger," he swears fiercely, "even if the bluddy roof drops on me." White-faced, his cap, clothes, boots and forearms all whitened by chalk, his lips and eyelids caked with dust, this ghostly figure fights on regardless of straining back and stiffening arm and shoulder muscles

*The authorities on Suffolk dialect, Forby, Moor and Claxton ignore this expression. Its meaning, sinking a shaft in stages on the slant, may be related to the term "bobby-hutch" defined by John Greaves Nall in his *Glossary of East Anglia*, 1866, as "a clumsy covered carriage or seat". The mine construction so called certainly provided seats for flints as they were hauled to the surface from "floorstone" level.

in a subterranean territory exclusively his own. Not just one flint difficult to dislodge affronts him but thousands — "bastards all."

This gruelling physical graft taxed his hardihood, with few relieving spells, from January to December. Providentially once he reached his pit's toe and packed himself into a burrow, a miner escaped whatever wintry furies raged above. He had, too, a refuge from blistering summer heat. The chalk walls, though cool, insulated him against draughts and preserved his body temperature. Though his toils demanded greater physical effort than knappers expended at their blocks, mining was healthier, even allowing for attacks of rheumatism caused by dampness in a pit's upper stages and the miner's tendency to cool off too quickly after hot work.

Arthur "Pony" Ashley with his single-pronged pick.
Sussex Archaeological Society

When they had to sink a new shaft, most men cut their first spit about 120 feet away from the old pit head. As a rule a stone digger reckoned on a week's work to excavate a new pit to "floorstone" level, forty to fifty feet below ground. Sometimes two diggers planned to meet down below by driving their burrows one towards the other. Once close enough to hear each other working, they hammered on the chalk and, guided by sound signals, finally threaded their burrows together. It must have been a fantastic meeting of mottled moles, each face peering out of a broken wall. Some extra space was then gained for storing unwanted chalk.

In hoisting his flint to the surface each digger worked to a pattern as traditional as it was arduous and time-consuming. "He would first raise his flint," said Herbert Edwards, "on to the staging nearest the toe; then with that staging loaded, he sprang up, using footholds in the chalk, and lifted his flint on to the next staging and so on. It might take half a dozen lifts to reach the top. He carried heavy lumps on his head, raising them first chest high against a wall; then ducking underneath, he headed up his flint platform by platform."

Some tabular slabs when grubbed out weighed two or three hundred-weights. Now and again, a massive chunk reached the top, but it was easier first to break it up into manageable proportions. The one assistant a digger might call on was a boy, usually a son, who helped him to raise his flint as well as collect and carry out loose chalk in buckets.

This pattern of flint mining ceased shortly before the 1939-45 War when Ashley, retired at last, went to live with his daughter in Doncaster, where he died. For two years after he gave up another Brandonian, Charlie Mail, a woodworker, carried on part-time operations on the heath. He set aside the practice of generations by installing a rough and ready haulage system of pulley, rope and bucket to raise his flints, powering it with an old motor-cycle engine. But although Mr Moreton, then a contractor, carted some loads of flints he had mined to the Edwards' knapping yard, his hauls, though of decent flint, did not amount to much. As the carpenter who built and erected a tripod for his tackle told me, he sank his shaft nearly straight down, not "on the sosh", and so ran into trouble.

Lingheath today offers us an enigmatic picture of sunlit, crop-bearing vistas which have supplanted these extraordinary mining activities, invisible except for circular impressions in the fields, irregularities in the corn, sudden subsidences, grassy mounds scattered with chalk and stone in wooded belts, and the few glaring holes left yawning in nearby Thetford Chase. If it were possible with some earth-penetrating electronic equipment to relay pictures from beneath the farmland's surface, one would see not so much a catacomb as series after series of disconnected shafts canalising into spiderish galleries, partially filled with debris or still hollow, but looking as if forsaken by some fantastically monstrous species of mole or earthworm.

Since Napoleon's brief hour, thousands of tons of top quality flint have been mined on Lingheath, every nodule of it prised out of its chalk mass by human hands and manhandled many times before its delivery to Brandon's knapping shops. Now only surface scars bear witness to all that herculean effort.

What joy, though, awaits archaeologists when, say, 4000 years hence they start to excavate and discover secrets hidden in this multi-tunnelled farm. May they not find some tools or broken bits of implements, perhaps a discarded iron-headed pick, a hammer's head, crowbar, food or tobacco tins, a smoker's clay pipe, beer bottles or cycle clips as remarkable in their eyes as artefacts abandoned by Neolithic man in the galleries at Grime's Graves? And, if they date their finds to the twentieth century, what conclusions will they draw about our civilisation?

Long before that the site could become an ancient industrial monument, with a few shafts and galleries opened up, and as much visited for its own interest as Grime's Graves today.

CHAPTER THREE

The Unveiling of Grime's Graves

THE story opens dimly when by some primeval shore, dried-up pebbly river bed or chalky ridge, a hairy biped suddenly bent down and picked up a flint. Was he attracted by a glint from it, a flash of translucence catching his wary eye? Or might he have stubbed a toe against a jagged edge? As he fingered the flint and ran his rough hand over its surface, possibly a grunt of satisfaction or snort of contempt flew from his lips.

Suppose he tossed the flint away, but saw that on falling it hit another flint, shattering it? Then some latent sense of curiosity brought the creature shuffling forward to pick up a fractured sliver. Now, as he tested its edge, he realised perhaps as one perceives the onset of daylight that he could do something with it, nudge, prod or stab a fellow creature, pierce an egg, a nut, a skull, cut up or scrape the fat off an animal skin.

We can only guess at flint's original inspiration to man, and at the first ideas it planted in his brain. The era when this tool-making itch burgeoned is again speculative, two to three million years ago being the age bracket archaeologists ascribe to simple flake pebble tools recovered from a floor occupied by hominids in the Olduvai Gorge, Tanzania.

Immensities of time glide by. Palaeolithic (Old Stone Age) cultures emerge, some confined to core tools, others to flake tools, those in the first category rounded or pear shaped as men trimmed a nodule to their design, those in the other category chipped from flakes, usually with flat backs.

Though man needed flint, stone and wood for weapons and tools, he lived as for ages past subjugated to his environment, seemingly powerless, lacking will to conquer or tame it but habituating himself to its seasons and rigours as glaciations advanced and receded. He killed and ate animals, birds and fish, even his fellow creatures, and, as a variation in diet or when unable to procure meat, he fed on what plants, berries or grubs he found edible. He made less impression on his habitat than herds of mammoths, bison, horses or deer. His foot and his appetite were lighter. If one reported on him like a schoolmaster, it might be said that he lacked ambition, was easily pleased, and should learn to think more constructively and act less on impulse. Nothing he did upset nature's balance. Flints endowed him not so much with extra muscle as with extra teeth.

Only amazingly late in his strangely resilient, tough-fibred story does a shift towards civilisation appear, at first a barely perceptible tilt. Man learned to cast spears with a thrower, thereby comprehending the principle of leverage. But it was more likely his use of bows and arrows, invented c.11,000 BC, that made him feel less restricted by his physique.

After centuries as a member of patriarchal groups, frequently on the move if not actually nomadic, Man began to settle in regions offering cave shelters and valleys rich in game. There he had security and scope to extend his hunting skills. Resorting to organised hunts, he rounded up and killed animals normally too swift or powerful for him to run down or tackle single-handed. As his success mounted, he improved his flint craft and with it the range of his activities and the utilisation of his resources and spoils.

The British Museum illustrates this gradual Stone Age transition in its permanent gallery, "Man Before Metals". One display of what are defined as Acheulean tools, 500,000 to 700,000 years old, includes a selection of quartzite choppers, cleavers and hand axes which are but rough-cut artefacts. They were found by Kalambo Falls, Zambia. The British eye must inevitably fasten on a display of flint hand axes and scrapers from the Middle Palaeolithic Age between 100,000 and 75,000 BC, for these implements originated from a large quarry at High Lodge, Mildenhall, nine miles from Brandon, where they were found during the second half of last century by brickearth diggers.

Through a succession of private collectors, their ownership passed to Dr W. Allen Sturge, a distinguished physician who, during his practice in Nice,

The seam of black flint or "floorstone" in a pit at Grime's Graves. *Brian Turner*

1881-1907, attended Queen Victoria and other members of the Royal Family holidaying on the Riviera. On his retirement in 1907 he bought Icklingham Hall, near Mildenhall, considering it an ideal centre from which to indulge his passion for collecting flint implements. There he built a museum and vase room, adding extensively to his treasures year by year until at his death in 1919 his collections contained 90,000 objects. He bequeathed both his home and foreign collections of early man's flint implements, assuredly the finest ever gathered together by a private person, to the British Museum. An item from his French collection, exhibited beside the Mildenhall artefacts, catches the eye for its sheer beauty; an elongated, superbly chipped, laurel-leaf-shaped point from Volgu, perhaps 75,000 years old.

Anyone tramping near where the Suffolk brickyard workers recovered these artefacts must be gripped by awareness of an enormous chasm in man's craftsmanship, so many thousands of years fumbling in his fire-lit darkness with flint a precious ally, but its true mystique eluding him.

Somewhere along the route of this slow progress from obscurity flint ushered in an era of savage domesticity. According to one theory someone, man or woman, took a splinter of bone, rounded it, using a serrated flint as a scraper, then burnished it with sandstone and ground one end to a point. Turning to the other end, the inventor took a microlith, a mere splinter of

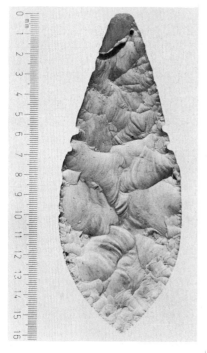

Left: The Ystradfellte dagger (c. 1800-1600 BC) with binding notches for hilt and blade area partially polished after flaking. This weapon was found in Brecknockshire.

National Museum of Wales, Cardiff

Opposite: A polished axe from Kentford in Suffolk, with a discoid knife found at Icklingham, some ten miles south of Brandon, and dated c. 1500 BC.

Moyses Hall Museum, Bury St Edmunds

flint, and drilled a hole—and lo, the world's first needle. Sinews provided ready-made thread, so animal hides could be stitched together for clothing or shelter coverings.

From the earliest times men collected flint from the ground at their feet, wherever it lay outcropped or was visible veined in chalk cliffs or fissures. As they learned to shape it more adroitly, their search for it became both discriminatory and intensive. At some period between 3500 and 2500 BC, communities began rejecting the weathered ultra brittle flint picked up on the earth's surface. By digging it raw out of chalk masses, they had material greater in tensile strength and superior in working quality.

Outcrops almost certainly afforded the first clues to flint seams lying underground, the veritable diamonds of the Neolithic fabricator's craft. Flints of peculiar colouring and texture, indigenous to a particular region, encouraged exploitation. Banded grey flint deposited at Krzemionki in Poland was exploited by miners who sunk more than a thousand mine shafts. This grey flint contrasts with the deep honey-coloured flint dug out at Le Grand Pressigny (Indre et Loire) in France, artefacts from which have been traced both in Jersey and Switzerland. Both these flint varieties stimulated man's aesthetic sense and provided the material for knives and double-headed axes used in ritual ceremonies.

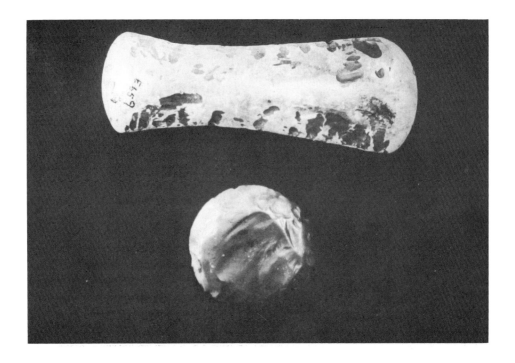

sand

boulder clay

flint nodules

soft chalk

hard chalk

flint nodules

topstone

wallstone

floorstone

flint nodules

Alan Sorrell '63

By the second millenia BC, flint mines had appeared in a wide range of cretaceous regions in Europe. The Neolithic miners in some districts tunnelled their shafts laterally from the point of outcrop into the hill's belly, as at Monte Tabuto in Sicily, but the more general practice, as followed at Aalborg in North Jutland, Rijkholt in the Netherlands and Spiennes in Belgium, consisted of excavating vertical bell-mouthed shafts, at the bottom of which the diggers pursued their flint seams in different directions. This method either spread to Britain or developed there independently.

Of East Anglian sites, Grime's Graves is unrivalled in Britain for size and complexity, but lesser workings in Neolithic times existed at Lynford, Great Massingham and Whitlingham, all Norfolk sites. In other English regions, there was a large complex at Cissbury Ring, just east of Findon on the Sussex Downs; mines, too, at Blackpatch Hill, three miles to the west; and, a mile beyond, at Harrow Hill; on Easton Down, about five miles north-east of Devizes, in Wiltshire; and on a small scale at Peppard Common, three miles west of Henley-on-Thames, in Oxfordshire.

The craftworker reacted inventively to better material, channelling his skills into new techniques. Whereas people of the Old Stone Age used hammerstones assumed to be about the size of cricket balls to crack flint into basic chopping tools, scrapers, knives and chisels, the men of the New Stone Age adopted both soft hammer flaking and pressure flaking for more elaborate work. They tapped or hammered a piece of bone, antler or hard wood against flint, dressing or chipping it neatly. Pressure flaking, almost a shaving process, highly delicate and sensitive in application, yielded ribbed and fluted work often artistic in elegance and symmetry.

As our ancestors dug the flint and trimmed it into axe heads, adzes, chisels, sickles and scrapers, and weapons such as spear and arrow heads, we can picture communities of about 2000 BC not hunting or raiding each other's settlements and carrying off or killing womenfolk but peacefully disposed. The skin-clad people, some wearing woven cloth, tended their plots of corn, mainly millet, harvesting it in due season by snipping off the ears with their hafted flint sickles. They then ground the grain into flour on their querns. Or they sat by their hearths, cutting up a freshly speared deer or slaughtered ox with flint knives and cleaning its skin with scrapers. "Cuts" then went into pots heated by red hot stones or roasted on log fires. Finally, eager to round off a sizzling meal with an extra tit-bit, someone grabbed a flint hammer and cracked a bone to extract its marrow.

Few sites preserved their ancient secrets for so long or cloaked them in so much mystery as Grime's Graves, sometimes defined as a Neolithic industrial

an Sorrell's reconstruction of Stone Age men raising flint from a pit at Grime's Graves.
Crown copyright reproduced with the permission of the Controller of HMSO

centre, at Weeting, 2½ miles from Brandon, on the Norfolk side of the Little Ouse River. For long elements of the supernatural haunted its face, guarded perhaps by the Norse deity, Grim. The site was seldom visited except by shepherds driving their flocks across Norfolk's warrens and heathlands. Villagers believed that demonic forces had punched the holes denting its surface. These depressions, some shallow, others low-pitched with chalk-scarred sides, intrigued and mystified reasonable men. One school regarded the site as a former Celtic settlement, each hollow indicating a hut floor where Boudica's Iceni had harboured before attacking their Roman oppressors in AD 61. The Rev. Francis Blomefield in his *History of Norfolk* (1739) advanced this explanation by 800-900 years. The site, as he understood it, had been a Danish encampment, semi-circular in shape and about twelve acres in extent.

The name itself fosters superstition, even dread. If, as some supposed, the term Grime, Grimme or Grim stood for witch, watersprite or devil, then Graves clearly had macabre or frightening undertones, though in this context the term is happily shudder-free since it derives from the German "Graben", pits or diggings. But for many generations Grime's Graves signified the "Devil's Hollows" into whose past or meaning it ill behoved one to pry. This tradition maligned the spot as a place apart, a hill tormented by and presided over by some demon.

A clergyman broke the spell. In the late 1860's that inveterate Yorkshire archaeologist, an inspired amateur, the Rev. (later Canon) William Greenwell, engaged some stone diggers from Brandon and started putting a spade to the site's hollows. For the first two seasons, his enterprise consisted of trial probes. Then in 1870 his diggers excavated a deep funnel-shaped pit which intersected different strata of flint. At the base galleries, cut into the rock-like chalk, branched off horizontally in several directions. From the debris in these cavities Greenwell and his assistants recovered some of the earliest mining tools used in Britain, shoulder blades of oxen and deer antler wedges and picks.

Neolithic miners, ignorant of metalwork, relied on red deer to furnish their picks, hacking off the antlers from stags out of velvet and killed in the hunt. There is a simple difference between cut or sawn off pedicles and those cast by living beasts, as in the former case the marks of severance show. Cast antlers, dropped after the autumn rut, might also have served if not too long exposed.

Miners easily converted an antler into a pick. They were interested only in what deerstalkers call the beam, the antler's main stem, and the brow tine, first stripping off the bez and trez tines either by burning or by cutting through their cortex with a flint saw. They also cut off the tip below the trez, and so acquired a surprisingly tough pick with a handle twelve to eighteen inches long.

The pitmen of Grime's Graves used these picks in great profusion,

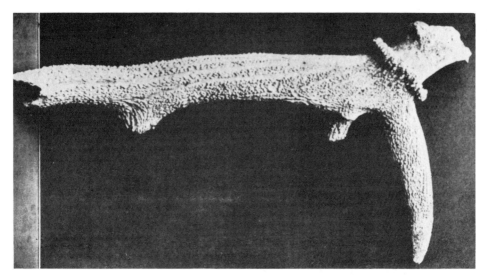

An antler pick with brow tine serving as its prong. The bez and trez tines have been removed and the tip shortened. *Prehistoric Society of East Anglia*

sometimes driving three or four into a chalk wall to lever out an obstinate nodule. They had, it seemed, an unlimited supply to call on. An estimated 25,000 red deer stags were either killed or contributed by natural discard their sets of antlers to this industry's labour force.

Unlike latter-day coal miners, the Neolithic miners never assaulted their raw material directly. Always they picked away at the chalk imprisoning the flint before prising it from its rock bed. If they dislodged a tabular slab too heavy to lift or an awkwardly shaped lump, they had no iron-headed hammer to crack it like the trousered stone diggers at Lingheath 4,000 years later, but they had to break it up, splitting it probably with a hammerstone, before they could transfer it to a chipping floor.

Of 244 deer antler picks recovered after one series of digs, a number were embedded with spicules, minute flint splinters, attesting their use as wedges or levers to loosen and grub out flints. Discoveries acquired a new dimension, almost as if one felt a handgrip from a sweating Neolithic workman, when some antler picks were seen to bear the palm prints of their users. Imagination wilts in musing over the survival potential of marks left by grubby, mud-stained hands.

Although Grime's Graves attracted specialist attention after Greenwell's excavations, archaeologists and others long differed in their conceptions of the area occupied and the time scale of activities there. A. Leslie Armstrong, a surveyor by profession and the principal excavator between the two World

Wars, first counted 346 cup-shaped depressions spread over approximately 34 acres. He believed the infilled pits had been worked intermittently over several millenia, say from 8000 to 2000 BC. He based his prediction on the discovery of a number of shallow pits on the hillside, mere funnelled-out hollows nine to fifteen feet deep, with steps cut roughly in their chalk sides. No lateral galleries diverged from their bottoms. The people who worked them used shoulder blades of aurochs and other animal bones for digging out the flint. Such open cast mining made few technical demands, and suggested to Armstrong an early period of exploitation.

It now appears that their working could have coincided with the Neolithic miner's ability to sink deep shafts on to the site's richest flint bed, the silky homogeneous black "floorstone". To reach it from near the crest of the Grime's Graves knoll, he dug straight shafts, their openings generous in circumference, the very antithesis of the narrow, one-man manageable holes cut out in staircase fashion by the miners of Lingheath.

Having opened up a large-mouthed shaft, the Neolithic worker bypassed, as he dug down, inferior seams of flint, the "topstone" and "wallstone", with sometimes intervening erratics, so-called potstones or paramoudras, an Erse term for sea-pears. And only when he dug into rock chalk did he straighten his

Red deer antler picks recovered from one of the pits at Grime's Graves before the First World War. At that period substantial trees gave the site shade and beauty.   *A. Leslie Armstrong*

shaft sides, knowing it would cause him no trouble, unlike the crumbly, friable stuff met with at higher levels. So, inch by inch, by scratch and scrape, he reached the precious "floorstone", ten to thirteen metres below the top. The seam was 20 to 30 cm. thick. Once he got to it, he collected at floor level every available nodule, and then struck off in horizontal directions, hewing out galleries of variable dimensions, from two and a half to seven feet wide, and averaging three feet in height.

No one will ever know how many hours an individual's stint lasted on a working day, or how many men, perhaps women too, exploited a pit. Lively speculation hinges also on the manner in which the flints were brought to the surface. The artist Alan Sorrell envisaged their raising by thongs and hide bag suspended from a log placed across the pit's mouth, the man at "floorstone" level heaving on the thong rope until his companion, manning the log, could retrieve the bag. Osier baskets might have been used. Again, miners might scramble up and down ladders, carrying flints by hand to pit top, or more laboriously travel up and down by their ropes.

Strikes, I guess, were unheard of in those times, but on at least one occasion Grime's Graves miners dropped their tools, even abandoned them, in obedience to some mystical power whose wrath they feared or whose bene-

The chalk goddess of Grime's Graves — an artist's impression of the tiny figurine, a fertility deity or a votive offering, now exhibited in the British Museum's "Man before Metals" gallery and dated c 2200 BC.

volence they desired to cultivate. In 1939 Armstrong entered a gallery where a tiny chalk figurine, amply proportioned like a pregnant woman, rested on an altar block of chalk, and nearby lay broken antler picks and a chalk phallus. Was the figurine a fertility goddess? Had her aid been invoked, perhaps by sacrifice, to lead the pitmen to a richer seam?

The British Museum dates this goddess of Grime's Graves of enigmatic potency to 2200 BC. A parallel exists with a hermaphrodite "God Dolly" carved out of ashwood, recovered from a timbered Neolithic trackway in the Somerset fens, and carbon dated c.2,900 BC. Both "ladies", perhaps conceived as votive offerings, now occupy the same showcase, almost back to back, in the British Museum.

In 1931, Grime's Graves passed into the custody of the Ministry of Works. Two pits, roofed over, were fitted with trap doors and metal ladders and made accessible for public inspection. Initially, you could descend with candles or torch and crawl along galleries radiating from their bases. But some visitors, starting off in a venturesome spirit, succumbed to feelings of claustrophobia, and children, excited or fearless, often both, tended to stray or get out of control. So such freedoms disappeared, and grilles caged in tunnel entrances. Despite these restrictions, the site year by year attracts more visitors than any other ancient monument or historic building in East Anglia. In 1960, the attendance figure was 10,800. During the next decade, with everyman becoming a car owner, that return looked meagre compared with the peak figure reached in 1974 of 49,173.*

In 1972 the British Museum, determined to find out everything possible about Grime's Graves, initiated the most comprehensive study of a Neolithic flint mining site so far undertaken anywhere. Working to a five-year plan, it set out to ascertain the site's true scale, its age, its yields, the racial grouping of communities exploiting its flint, their technical methods, the use and distribution of their products, skeletal remains, botanical deposits and so forth.

The team, led by Mr G. de G. Sieveking and Dr I. H. Longworth of the Department of Prehistoric and Romano-British Antiquities, called on specialist assistance from the museum's research laboratory and many outside individuals and institutions, including the Prehistoric Mining Group of the Netherlands Geological Society, some of whose members, mining engineers and geologists, had worked in Dutch coalfields during the 1939-45 War.

Vertical air cover disclosed ploughed-out mine shafts. The known site and its surroundings were surveyed by black and white and infra-red photography from the most effective height, 410 metres. Mr A. J. Clark, of the Ancient Monuments Laboratory, supervised magnetic surveys, and Mrs A. Millett, formerly of the Oxford Research Laboratory for Archaeology, organised resistivity surveys. Soil when compact conducts electricity readily, but any disturbance in the soil will affect the way in which an electric current is passed,

---

*Official record of visitors to Grime's Graves for the last five years of the 1970's is: 1975, 49,077; 1976, 46,000; 1977, 47,345; 1978, 36,550 and 1979, 18,316, the steep drop resulting from closure of the inspection pit during the summer months for repairs to conform with national safety regulations.

sand pockets, air pockets and other features disturbing the natural con-
ductivity of the soil. Resistivity meters can be used to measure and record
reactions indicating disturbance within the ground.

Through these and other tests, the mining site at Grime's Graves is now
known to extend over a minimum of 93 acres, in contrast to the 12 defined by
Parson Blomefield, 21 by Canon Greenwell and 34 by A. L. Armstrong.

During the first three years of research, the museum's team opened up
four deep pits out of a total of 600 infilled shafts, a number of which were open
cast workings three to four metres wide. The four selected varied in depth
from ten to thirteen metres. From one the investigators, assisted by working
parties of Borstal boys, removed 600 tons of rubble or infilling. Specialists
sifting this debris identified items of pottery and animal bones, several of cows,

An enlarged section of an antler
pick showing fingerprints left by
a Neolithic miner.
Prehistoric Society of East Anglia

left either by the miners or by occupiers of the site at later dates. That
particular pit when worked out would have yielded, it was calculated, about
eight tons of raw flint, the aggregate of hauls from its shaft and radial galleries
with their bays or apses.

No fewer than 500 antler picks were recovered from a single pit. The red
stags foraging in the region in Neolithic times, roaring their challenges by
autumnal dawns or crashing through the undergrowth, grew finer sets of
antlers than the eighteen, twenty or twenty-two pointers conserved in Thetford
Chase today, lordly beasts, as they are, superior in weight and conformation to
the crag-scaling sinewy wild deer of the Scottish Highlands. Breckland's
prehistoric stags apparently fed better and grew thicker beams, equalling if
not surpassing in monarchical splendour the thirty pointers shot by Herman
Goering in German deer forests.

A number of picks, some well muddied when used, retained after 4000
years the palm prints and sometimes the fingerprints of their Neolithic users.

Among the oldest visible marks left by human hands, craftsmen's hands at that, they deserve to be locked away in some nuclear-proof store. Twenty picks bearing such impressions have been examined by Dr Nigel Seeley, of London University's Laboratory of Archaeology, in an attempt to discover the racial affiliations of communities mining the site.

Through radio carbon dating, it has become clear that the greatest activity at Grime's Graves took place from 2000 to 1800 BC, although pioneer flint-seekers probably started digging there 500 years earlier, and some mining continued until the fifteenth century BC.

The Dutch mining engineers found evidence in the galleries of procedures closely related to those adopted in modern coalfields. When they sunk deep shafts, the Neolithic miners clearly worked with specialist knowledge, systematically disposing of unwanted chalk or rubble and, as if schooled in load-bearing capacities, knowing precisely how wide and high to tunnel without walls collapsing or roofs falling. Having sunk a shaft, they went only a certain distance from its base in a straight line, first tunnelling a narrow gallery, at the end of which they quarried an apse or bay, and then working

An archaeologist records the discovery of an antler in a pit at Grime's Graves during excavations in the 1970s. *British Museum*

backwards towards the shaft's open-to-the-sky bottom, creating fresh bays and piling up unwanted chalk in those already stripped of flint. Extracting the flint, whether nodular or tabular, they habitually worked from above the seam, picking out the chalk sitting on top of it. Wall pressures then bore directly, like the base of an arch, on the flint stratum. Sometimes there was a thin layer of soft clay running above the nodules which helped to ease their release.

Not only did the Neolithic miners show a remarkable understanding of stresses and pressures, particularly as to how much chalk could be excavated without disaster, but their preference for working the "floorstone" from above is considered superior from a mining standpoint to the practices of nineteenth and twentieth century miners at Lingheath, who first dug underneath the flint.

Miners ancient and modern had this in common. All, tapping or hammering away at rock-like chalk, appreciated the advantage of sharp-pointed picks. You cannot sharpen an antler tine as you can an iron-headed pick. So once his pick became blunt, the Neolithic workman wanted a new one, perhaps a fresh antler pick each day, to judge by the enormous number of discards.

An Australian engineer once asked me why the depressions or hollows marking pit mouths lie so close together. If the miners ventured far in horizontal lines from a shaft's bottom, they would be wasting flint. Suppose they cut out narrow galleries in four directions, say the cardinal points; the farther they extended these tunnels the greater the intervening area, so sensibly, they restricted their minings to chalk which could support it, leaving only small amounts of flint in between their tunnels.

They used no pit props or supports. Yet in a world where life was perhaps nasty, brutal and short, there is little evidence of accidents. The museum's researches turned up few human remains, but in one gallery the skeleton of a small Neolithic dog (canis domesticus), about cairn size, was found surrounded by flints as if buried there with appropriate gravestones by an affectionate owner.

Earlier investigators concluded that the miners used chalk lamps fuelled with animal fats to illuminate their diggings. This latest five-year study, though, revealed no traces of lamp black besmirching any gallery wall. Here and there chalk patches were rubbed smooth, as though fibrous clothing might have polished the chalk as miners crawled by.

"It's quite wrong," Mr Sieveking said, "to suppose that the principal product of Grime's Graves was the flint axe. That was true of Cissbury (150 shafts) where flint mining took place 1000 years earlier, say 3,300 BC, and at Easton Down in Wiltshire (253 shafts) where mining began 750 years earlier.

"As a pure guess I would put the number of flint axes made from Grime's

Graves flint in any one year at 20,000, and regard the flint axe as representing not more than twenty per cent of the site's output of flint implements."

Evidence points to mining at Grime's Graves being a seasonal occupation, pursued perhaps from May to September, though a community might have started opening up a shaft at winter's tail end. Shafts, once opened, needed to be worked out before winter. If left open, they would be repositories for all sorts of wild creatures. When the museum's investigators, of necessity, left a pit open throughout winter, their first task on re-entering it was to clean it of stinking carcases of rats, rabbits, bats, voles, moles, toads and other creatures. A more cogent reason for not letting winter get into a shaft lay with its penetration. Flint, if exposed to frost, becomes even more unworkable than when over-heated. Its texture breaks up. It flakes erratically.

It can never be known how much flint mined at Grime's Graves was wholly or partly finished on chipping floors beside the pits, nor whether, as in France in historic times, the men who excavated the flint also knapped it. A fair tonnage of Grime's Graves black flint could have been transported raw or as "rough-outs" for finishing or polishing by communities domiciled many miles away. Again, we have few clues as to what goods, services or stock were exchanged for this coveted material.

Where the miners lived is also not clear. Probability points to their huts or shelters standing near if not beside the Little Ouse River, about a mile from the pits. Apart from needing a water supply, some Neolithic people surely craved for a bite of fish if only to give their palates relief from the inescapable venison! Who were they? How many were engaged in mining in any one season? So many questions beg the museum's elucidation. Ultimately the results of its multi-faceted investigations are expected to occupy twelve volumes. But, despite so much unveiling by experts, I shall be surprised if some mystery does not still envelop the site.

For the time being, with its fieldwork concluded, the museum has no plans for further research there. "Because of its earlier occupation," Mr Sieveking said, "it would be interesting at a later stage to investigate Cissbury and discover in what ways practices there differed from those at Grime's Graves."

Visitors need no longer feel apprehensive about taking a look at this black flint seam, and at the galleries tunnelled at its level. In the interest of safety and security, the Department of the Environment has covered in the one mineshaft open for their inspection. The single descent/ascent ladder is firmly fixed, and all who use it must wear helmets. Now if any lady in descending plants her foot on the head of the man below her in mistake for a rung, no harm should befall him.

CHAPTER FOUR

Strike-a-lights, Medieval Flushwork and Gunflints

INSIDE a showcase of knapping equipment, gunflints and photographs at the superbly square-flint-faced Bridewell Museum in Norwich, a repository of Norfolk's industrial crafts, a printed notice declares: "Flint may have been mined and worked continually at Brandon since Neolithic times. Brandon knappers were responsible for the flint work of many of Norfolk's finest churches."

Though centuries roll by, civilisations rise and topple, at no time did flint pass out of production or men cease to work it skilfully, despite their preoccupation with metals, new crafts and new techniques. Iron Age tribes collected cobblestones and erratics from local gravel as floors for their wattle huts. Their hill forts with ditches and extensive earthworks sometimes had an inner wall or rampart of flint as a final bastion against attackers. In their turn, the Romans packed flints in layers, sometimes twenty-one feet wide, in constructing their road systems. The Roman *agger* or embankment built to carry light traffic rested on a foundation of big stones, well rammed down, with often a single layer of small stones or flints on top; it drained well. They also split flints, but relied mainly on raw stones in building their massive coastal or river forts such as Burgh Castle at the north-east tip of Suffolk, with walls bonded in flint and tiles eleven feet wide at the base and fifteen feet high, absorbing hundreds of tons of stone, probably all gathered and applied by native craftsmen.

It is regrettable that Brancaster (Branodunum) has disappeared. The walls of this fort of the Saxon Shore that once guarded the Wash against pirates were demolished to build a malthouse, and, perhaps by a stroke of historical justice, the malthouse has also disappeared. But as Professor J. K. S. St Joseph, of Cambridge University's Committee for Aerial Photography, told me: "Aerial photographs taken over the last few years show that there are buried remains of internal buildings at Brancaster. None of these has been excavated; it might well prove that they were built partially in flint, but that is anyone's guess."

In the summer of 1936 Professor St Joseph undertook a brief excavation of the Roman fort, the results of which he published in the *Antiquaries*

Journal. "In our main section," he said, "nothing of the fort wall remained in position, but we also uncovered the angle tower at the NW corner. This was built in ashlar (blocks of limestone, I think); only the bottom two or three courses remained in position. We encountered no walling in flint."

However, knapped flints appeared in facings of town walls at St Albans, Caistor-by-Norwich and other centres.

Such building skills lapsed when the Saxons poured into eastern Britain, for these people of the dark Germanic woods built fundamentally in timber with wattle-and-daub infilling, using thatch for their roofs. But confronted by

A bird-headed firesteel discovered in a grave at Brighthampton, Oxfordshire, in the nineteenth century. This piece is dated to the mid-fifth century by similar finds made in a rich grave at Krefeld in Germany.   *Ashmolean Museum, Oxford*

sea raiders even more ruthless and land hungry than themselves, they fell back on stouter materials for a defensive system and built round watchtowers of flint with entrances placed high above ground. Hard to burn, hard to destroy, but blessed, indeed elevated, by time, numbers of these once-isolated outposts survive as church bell towers in Norfolk and Suffolk.

Throughout history, and of course earlier, the human race has needed fire for warmth, comfort and light as well as for manufacturing weapons and implements in bronze and iron, and also for clearing forests to win new land for cultivation and settlement. So the strike-a-light, a flint used to strike off fiery particles from iron, performed a daily service whether lighting a lamp, a candle, a cooking fire or a metalsmith's forge. Flints recovered from grave goods attest their value to ancient peoples both as contemporary and after-life necessities.

Mr David Brown, of the Department of Antiquities at the Ashmolean Museum, Oxford, in his account *Firesteels and Pursemounts Again* published in the *Bonner Jahrbuch, 1977,* analyses the structure, condition and accessories of a large number of pursemounts, plain and buckled, recovered from Anglo-Saxon graves. Thirty-one of the buckled kind had flints associated with them. Such evidence, apart from worn steels, convincingly supports his theory that pursemounts, part of the funeral furniture of influential Anglo-Saxons, were in effect firesteels, the purse containing the inflammable material and perhaps the flint, its iron base the surface off which sparks were ripped, and its ornamentation or jewellery a symbol of the owner's rank or status.

A stylised bird-headed firesteel, recovered from a woman's grave at Holywell Row, Mildenhall, in 1930, assuredly marks her as a superior lady. A few broken strike-a-lights* were excavated recently from the Anglo-Saxon cemetery at Morning Thorpe, about ten miles south of Norwich, but this material, when I inquired about it, was still undergoing examination by the Norwich Survey at the Centre of East Anglian Studies, University of East Anglia.

Not everyone accepts the civilising influences which many specialists today attribute to the Viking invasions of the British Isles. Among the less barbaric of their violent actions, they set fire to Saxon homesteads with flint and steel. Later on, in fairness, it must be said that the same combination enabled them as farming settlers, living under tight laws, a political and monetary system, to exploit the land and settle their craftsmen in embryonic towns.

The strike-a-light, though it passed in time into the tinder box, underwent little change as a knapped oval or shoe-shaped flint. But its containers evolved into elaborately decorated boxes and pistol representations, some designed as gifts for royalty, a widely researched and detailed record of which appears in M. Christy's catalogue of exhibits in the Bryant and May Museum of fire-making appliances.

To return to those controversial Vikings whose civilising aspirations sprang from such cruel practices, the superior vitality of these sea rovers and colonisers may be reflected in Domesday Book, 1086. Suffolk, split up into twenty-four and a half hundreds or divisions, then returned an estimated population of 20,491, of whom 7,460 were freemen — more than half the total of freemen recorded in the entire survey. Successful raiders were not serf material. The spirit of independence, so consolidated, still outcrops in the East Anglian breed.

Brandon, where a tiny Neolithic settlement might once have existed, at this period acknowledged Ely Abbey as its overlord. The abbey's manor there consisted of five carucates of land, a carucate being about 120 acres, whose occupiers, bondsmen all, being bound to the abbey, numbered eight villeins, four bordars and seven serfs. They worked three ploughs. There were two acres of meadows, one fishery and a church with thirty acres attached to it. Priests counted as freemen, though their allegiance was tied. The animal

---

*Though strictly speaking, a strike-a-light is a flint, an iron strike-a-light shown at the British Museum's Exhibition *The Vikings* (1980) came from a grave at Marstein in Oppland, South Norway, and was probably the counterpart of many such devices used by Vikings in ravaging and settling in the British Isles.

census amounted to two asses, eleven beasts (cattle), two hundred sheep and twenty swine. The settlement, said to be one league long by half a league wide, covered about 720 acres, and was straddled by wild expanses of woodland and scrubby heath.

Flints, so readily accessible in East Anglia, were much in demand as building material for abbeys, castles, churches, shire halls and manor houses. But not until the fourteenth century did its decorative qualities begin to excite interest. The following century saw an extraordinary flowering of architectural grace in which flint flushwork and chequered panelling, embodied in so many medieval buildings, uplifted one's line of sight, as it still does five centuries later.

Shrines of soaring elegance abound. It is hard to particularise. Canon John Fitch, a great lover of Suffolk churches, their history, beauty and treasures, recommended for particular study the flint work at Southwold,

Left: The porch of St Mary's Church, Woodbridge, in which knapped flint infillings greatly enhance the ornamental grace of the building.

Terry Moore

Opposite: The gatehouse of Butley Priory, built 1320-25. Above the gateway stands a remarkable heraldic panel with thirty-five coats of arms arranged in five rows.

Terry Moore

Laxfield, Eye, Gipping, Long Melford and Lavenham. To this selection, I would add St Mary's, Woodbridge, expressive like the others in the controlled artistry and varied designs of its knapped flint. Anyone touring Suffolk with those churches in mind is assured of aesthetic delight, quite apart from their religious significance and the hallowed stillness of their interiors.

An acute critic of civilisation's heritage, Lord Clark, has admitted being captivated by flint textures in Suffolk. In his words: "The use of this magical material reaches a high point at Butley Priory and Gipping, where flint work is used with the precision of the inlaid marbles of the Taj Mahal. In the famous Priory gatehouse, flints produce a rich precious texture unique in the architecture of the world."

Norfolk does not lag behind Suffolk for fine flushwork in its medieval buildings. Strangers from many countries gather in little groups admiring the walls of three of Norwich's most eminent ancient buildings, the Bridewell

Museum, the Guildhall and the church of St Michael-at-Coslany (St Miles). The Bridewell, built as a private house late in the fourteenth century, retains on its north wall flints agelessly locked together, an almost perfect and continuous example of what William Arderon, FRS, found in 1729 while investigating Norwich's old buildings, "some of the flints being cut exactly square and so curiously formed as not to admit a knife's blade between them."

For seekers after more subtle designs in flint there is that gem of a building, the Guildhall, at one end of the city's gaudily canopied market square. The hall was founded about 1410, and its east end, rebuilt in 1535, houses the Council Chamber, the exterior glory of which lies in the wall beneath the clock tower, its base a solid phalanx of flint squares, and above it, in Sir Nikolaus Pevsner's telling phrase, "the gayest, almost carnavalesque (sic) diaper flushwork".

Many of Norfolk's parish churches also exhibit flint craft at its best. One may be forgiven for thinking the stone imperishable, but the lime mortar binding it into walls does not wear too well, especially when the gap between flints and mortar is far wider than knife blade thickness. Medieval craftsmen knew the art of positioning flints securely in this mortar, setting it well back. The wisest of their modern successors takes a stick to dig in or indent this mortar and so decrease its exposure to wind, sun and frost.

It cannot be established with certainty whether flint workers from Brandon travelled the region like guilds of woodworkers from the monasteries setting forth to carve bench heads, misericords or other items of church furniture. Two contracts survive from the Middle Ages for erecting church towers in Suffolk. Two masons, described as Richard Russel of Donewich (Dunwich) and Adam Powle of Blythburgh, who undertook to build Walberswick Tower, 1425, with walls six feet thick, were provided with "freeston, lyme and Calyon, water and Soond"; (Calyon, a term of old French origin and spelt variously in documents as kaylowe, calyou, calion and caliou, indicated as a rule flint pebbles). Except for the first year, the masons were contracted to build only from Lady Day to Michaelmas, but if that year was set aside for cutting the stone nothing was said about it.

The agreement for Helmingham Church, 1488, is more specific. The master mason, Thomas Aldrych, of North Lopham, Norfolk, was given ten years in which to raise a tower sixty feet high with "a black wall wroughte of flynt". He was expected to be economical in his use of black flint and freestone, but his terms contained no reference to the knapping required. This, presumably, was left to his own skills or discretion. Similarly, no instructions about working the flint appear in the seventeenth century agreement for Gislingham. As John Harvey in his *Medieval Crafts* says of East Anglian flushwork, "there is nothing to suggest that the work was done by a distinct branch of the trade."

The east end of the Guildhall, Norwich. Above the solid base of squared flints the knapped flint of the upper section almost dances in its chiaroscuro setting.
Terry Moore

Evidence is scanty and scattered. So few documents, least of all wills, refer to craftsmen who shaped and cut flint for medieval flushwork, used flint to piece together sacred monograms, petitions to saints, inscriptions commemorating notable benefactors and other literary designs embodied in walls, or indeed adapted flint for decorative effect of any kind.

The world altered at a slow pace in medieval days. But man's devilish ingenuity scarcely ever rested. Tirelessly he brought out new and deadlier weapons with which to destroy his fellows. Archers retained their status, and practice at the butts for the most part remained compulsory in Elizabeth's "Golden Age", but already calivers or hand-guns were coming into vogue as birding pieces for sportsmen and personal weapons for militiamen.

The comic genius of Shakespeare fastened on this development in *The Merry Wives of Windsor* when he hid Falstaff in the house of Mistress Ford. The return of the lady's husband is expected at any moment. His brothers guard the doors with pistols. At first there is talk of concealing the old reprobate up the chimney. But this idea is quickly scotched. It might have caused a shattering denouement for, as Mistress Page remarks: "There, they always discharge their birding pieces." A noisy but felicitous scene marked the homecoming of hunters. Weary from a hard day's chase and with guns loaded, they no sooner get inside than as a safety precaution they go to their chimneys, push up their gun muzzles and blast off. Heaven knows how much soot descended, or whether chimney sweeps were ever needed.

At intervals European sovereigns presented one another with rare and costly gifts as peace or goodwill offerings, but sometimes with the malefic intent of concealing political stratagems. It is doubtful, though, if any double dealing or dark motives entered into the gift of "foure fowling pieces with there furniture very richly garnished and inlaid with plates of gold" which James I sent to Philip III of Spain in 1604.

We simply do not know when or where flints were first used to spark off gun charges, nor the country of the inventor's origin. Among the earliest hand-guns to use a flint was a wheellock, operated on the coiled spring system, its tension controlled by a crank form of clockwork. When the weapon was fired, the wheel rotated against a flint, sparks flying off.

In 1585 Julius, Duke of Brunswick, experimented with iron pyrites collected by his retainers from near Seefen. In breaking up fragments to fire his guns, he "often bruised his fingers and was advised by his physicians not to expose himself to the sulphurous vapours of their substance." Though

A musketeer and his match, an engraving from Jacob de Gyeyn's *Maniement d'Armes,* Amsterdam, 1608.

pyrites, unlike flint, engender sparks when struck, their nauseating fumes may have encouraged inventors to look for cleaner methods of firing guns and brought flint to the fore. However, Germany is not rich in chalk-bearing flint. That possibly explains why soldiers of the Duchy of Brunswick were not equipped with flintlocks in place of matchlocks until 1687. The latter firearm depended for its efficiency on a slow-burning fuse gripped between jaws at the end of a pivoted arm or serpentine. Once a musketeer lit his match, he wanted an immediate engagement or the certainty of fine weather if the battle was prolonged. For his fuse, which was a long impregnated tape, smouldered on, and was horribly vulnerable to rain. For fear he might run out of fire, he sometimes lit it at both ends.

Authorities credit France with inventing the flintlock about 1600. Fated to be the primary infantry weapon for more than 250 years, it initiated a mighty new era for flint as a lethal instrument. A fragment of flint screwed into the gun's cock and held there under tension plunged forward when the trigger was pulled. The flint struck the frizzle, a soft steel plate, and tore off a stream of white hot steely particles which tumbled into the priming pan. Its powder flashed, the flame leapt through a touchhole and exploded the gun's charge.

Early flintlocks were called snaphaunces, a term sometimes attributed to the Dutch "snap haens", which means "chicken thief", as the flint's action suggested a quick snatch. A more plausible theory attributes the term to the German "Schnapphahn" (pecking hen), because the gun's cock, with a flint clamped in it, pecks forward on to the steel to rip sparks off it.

With snaphaunces, sometimes written snaphances, the steel or frizzle was independent of the pan cover. Soldiers swivelled the cover to one side before firing. This movement might occupy a fatal split second, and in foul weather water could drip off the barrel into the powder and render the gun useless. To avoid such disadvantages, locksmiths evolved what is often recognised as the true flintlock, a firearm whose combined steel and pan cover is struck and knocked open by the flint.

The Miquelet gunlock introduced to France from Spain about 1625 also used a flint or stone to provoke the vital sparks. But nowhere in France, Spain or England has evidence emerged to suggest that at this period a manufactured flint was used.

In the Civil War period matchlocks were mainly in use, but because of obvious danger from the burning match, guardians of the powder usually had flintlocks. Commonwealth forces in Ireland under command of Lieutenant-General Michael Jones consisted of "horse, foot and dragoons". The arms of the "horse" or cavalry element were a sword and pair of flintlock pistols for each trooper; the foot or infantry were divided into pikemen and musketeers, and the dragoons, a sort of mounted infantry, had swords and firelocks (snaphaunces).

Of significance, not only for its early date, is a Board of Ordnance document dated 26th September, 1654, in which the Commissioner for the Admiralty and Navy orders the taking into store of 10 tons of flintstones, 4,000 powder horns, 1,000 horseshoes, 2,000 horseshoe nails and other accessories "lately returned from the sea." Were, at this time, the flintstones already knapped? Troop commanders probably instructed their artificers (farriers or carpenters) to take charge of available flints and if need be to knock them into shape for servicing the troop's firearms. But would even the astutest Ironside have insisted on flints of prime quality, well-shaped and of proven durability as spark-raisers?

It was not until 1719 that manufactories for gunflints first attracted historical interest in France, although there, as in England and elsewhere, such enterprises were of earlier origin. According to surviving documents, London gunsmiths received orders in 1661 and 1662 to provide King Charles's garrisons in Tangier and Ireland with deliveries of 5,000 and 10,000 "flint-stones cutt", and in November 1685, the Board of Ordnance agreed to accept "20,000 flints for Pistolls, Carbines and Musquetts". Nothing was said about sizes, but it looks as if flints were already being manufactured to different patterns since on 22nd December that year the Board, with the Master-General present, gave orders for "flints 300 of sorts" to be delivered and apportioned to the King's Armouries at Whitehall and St James's.

In much of its correspondence and minutes, the Board prefers the spelling "musquet" or "musquett" to the plain English "musket", and flints are purchased at so much per mille, abbreviated p.m., instead of the English "per thousand".

The Board was reorganised by Charles II a short time before his death in 1685. The peer serving as its Master-General, who might on occasion be a Field-Marshal, had the assistance of a Lieutenant General and Surveyor General, but was personally responsible to the sovereign for equipping the army and navy with every species of "infernal machine" and all munitions and stores needed for battle efficiency. The office also carried responsibility for fortifications, artillery and engineers. As head, therefore, of the nation's first permanent military department, the Master-General was not only concerned with all "ordnance, emption and munition" but with the testing and acceptance of new weapons and equipment as well as the hard core of the nation's coastal defences at home and abroad.

Lesser duties were laid on him such as the organisation of firework displays celebrating national victories or royal birthdays, and provision of armour for the King's Champion, including payment of the bill tendered before Coronations for its repainting. At one period, he appointed the "Astronomical Observator" at Greenwich, whose job was "to apply himself with most exact care and diligence to rectify the tables of Motions of the

These three photographs show the action of the flintlock. The weapon is a Kentucky pistol owned by Mr Neville Offord, of Bury St Edmunds, who knapped his own flint. At top the pistol is fully cocked; in the second picture the flint is striking the frizzle or steel, which is knocked upwards allowing the resulting sparks to fall into the pan to ignite the priming powder.

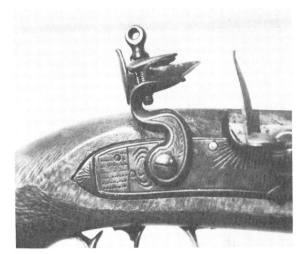

Musketeers of the Honourable Artillery Company firing their matchlocks in the grounds of Armoury House, London.

Honourable Artillery Company

Heavens and the Places of the Fixed Stars . . . for perfecting the Art of navigation."

Warlike stores for the Navy called for just as much forethought and administration as those required by the Army. In 1676, an expedition fitted out for Virginia was issued with 300 matchlocks and 200 snaphaunces. Four years later another expedition with Tangier as its destination took on board 1,000 matchlocks and 700 snaphaunces. In each case the snaphaunces required flints.

By 1684, if not earlier, those in charge of the Navy drew up tables of arms, including flint allocations, for fighting ships of specified cannon strength. The leviathans, mounting 100 cannon, were each allowed 4,000 flints for their entitlement of 150 snaphaunce muskets, ten musquetoons (large bore, short muskets sometimes charged with thirty bullets), ten blunderbusses and forty pistols. Ships at the bottom end of the scale, with 24 cannon, received 400 flints as spark raisers for thirty snaphaunce muskets, five musquetoons and six pistols.

At about this period, gunflint manufacturing businesses began supplying arsenals controlled by the Board of Ordnance either directly or through London gunsmiths or hardware merchants. In Queen Anne's reign, if only to keep the Duke of Marlborough happy, craftsmen applied their hammers to flints excavated from chalk quarries in several parts of England to produce gunflints of different sorts for the Duke's armies. At this stage, however, there is no evidence of Brandon's entry into the trade.

In 1727 the Hanover War Chancery sent a cadre of German artificers to England to learn our flint craft, but whatever skills they acquired during their attachment came to an abortive end, because the stone available on their return, so-called horn-stone, did not knap effectively.

The craft grew up almost imperceptibly, though early in the flintlock's life sportsmen as well as soldiers had cause to curse the gunsmith's latest model if the flint screwed into its cock failed to beget a stream of steely sparks.

In his *Animadversions of Warre* (1639) Robert Ward detailed maintenance tasks for owners of Dog-lock or English pistols. After describing procedures for "Bend your Cocke" and "Guard your Cocke", he came to "Order your Hammer" and wrote: "You are gently to draw down your steele upon the pan with your right hand, provided always there be a good flint and that it be a good flint, and that it be evenly measured, less it under or over reacheth which may hazard the firing."

His appreciation recognises the flint's importance as a vital factor in fire control. But how often was it overlooked, and how disastrously or tragically? For about 200 years fine old English and Scottish gentlemen, as opposed to French or German nobility, settled their differences with pistols in preference to sabres or swords. Many a duellist, keeping a dawn rendezvous, was humiliated if not grievously injured or killed because the flint in his pistol was badly adjusted, broke on hitting the steel or was of too poor a quality to rip off sparks. Ill-flinted pistols might be triggered off a dozen times without a discharge.

For warfare, good flints shaped to fit specific weapons would have been indispensible, the needs of men thrown into battle by land or sea far overshadowing those of acrimonious individuals, however eminent. As military realists, the French banned the export of gunflints from major manufacturing regions such as Champagne and Picardy when campaigns were planned. Incidentally their *caillouteurs* (stone cutters) at chalk/flint-bearing sites knapped with a "roulette", a disc-headed hammer, and cut the flint against a chisel-like point, a technique different from that of English knappers. But once embargoes were lifted, the Dutch jumped in, their merchants buying up French stocks avidly to hold them until they found quartermasters eager for supplies at their price.

Did a reflection of this arms traffic come to light on 21st December, 1797, when the Office of Ordnance at the Castle of Good Hope took in an enormous quantity of Dutch equipment from Commissary Williamson? Among a large collection of muskets, wallpieces (fixed but swivelling musquetoons), carbines, blunderbusses, pistols, fuses, balls, moulds and so forth, the ordnance clerk listed 18,830 flints for wallpieces, 22,819 musket flints, 20,271 carbine flints and 39,007 pistol flints. Numerically this flint haul exceeded the intake of cartridges and loose ball.

From 1700 to 1815, the flintlock known as Brown Bess, subject to modifications, served as the British Army's musket. Our martial poet, Rudyard Kipling, celebrated its deadliness with a verse of seven stanzas, the first of which ran:

> In the days of lace ruffles, perukes and brocade
> Brown Bess was a partner whom none could despise—
> An outspoken, flinty-lipped, brazen-faced jade,
> With a habit of looking men straight in the eyes—
> At Blenheim and Ramillies fops would confess
> They were pierced to the heart by the charms of Brown Bess.

However shrewdly the Duke of Marlborough understood flint lore in master-minding his famous victories, the young General James Wolfe, it is clear, trusted implicitly in the flints cocked in his infantry's muskets. In June, 1759, after the Navy by superlative seamanship had landed his army at Isle d'Orleans, four miles from Quebec, he began harassing the French by feints and skirmishes to deceive their commander, Montcalm, about his real intentions. One such piece of strategy ran into bad weather, the French positions being strongly held as Wolfe's grenadiers, without adequate cover, stormed the French cliffside redoubt but were hurled back, clawing at rocks slippery with blood and rain, their powder wet and muskets unfireable.

No misadventure impeded Wolfe's main assault, carried out on 13th September after another *ruse de guerre*. He selected the cove at Anse de Foulon, a mile and a half above Quebec, for his breakout. His vanguard, put ashore there in darkness, scaled a 175-foot cliff and quickly overpowered a light defence post on the cliff top. Before dawn, Wolfe had his fighting force of about 4,500 men drawn up on the Heights of Abraham, with the advantage of an open battleground.

This daring penetration threw Montcalm off his guard. He reacted, historians say, too impetuously, determining at once to push the English back over the cliffs, dead or alive. Wolfe deployed his redcoats in a thin line, two deep, their Brown Besses made ready. The French advanced, first steadily, then at a run, but firing raggedly, their ranks unbroken by a single British musket ball. On they came. Then, when they were no more than forty yards away, the muskets of Wolfe's battle line blazed, one volley, two—each almost as effective as modern machine-gun fire—followed by a bayonet charge. Quebec, the key to Canada, was won. English gunflints, useless in one skirmish, helped to make a devastating impact in the crucial battle.

CHAPTER FIVE

Brandon's Emergence as a Gunflint Centre

A NEW epoch that many hoped would revolutionise the manufacture and supply of British arms began on 30th March, 1782, when Charles Lennox, third Duke of Richmond, took office as Master-General of the Ordnance. Inheriting his title as a 15-year-old, the Duke revelled in action, was mercurial in temperament and little disposed to compromise. General Wolfe admired him. For some years Edmund Burke valued his qualities, like his friendship, highly; then, becoming less enthusiastic, he chided him for dissipating his mind "in too great a variety of minute pursuits, all of which from the natural vehemence of your temper you follow with almost equal passion."

The Duke shone in debate with a hard aggressive brilliance epitomised by his counter to a parliamentary opponent, "Nobility will not be browbeaten by an insolent minister."

Secret trials held in Hyde Park to test different patterns of musket probably reinforced his earlier impressions of flint's role in a gun's efficiency. A resolute commander, though apt to quarrel with his juniors, he showed dash and bravery in leading a regiment of the line at Minden (1759), and by the end of the Seven Years War had attained major-general's rank. For a short period in 1765, he was British Ambassador Extraordinary at the Court of Louis XV in Paris. Of significance also, he inherited a small French estate at Aubigny where he frequently spent his summers, to the dismay of parliamentary colleagues needing his counsel in London. So, while on official duty or enjoying his recreation in that country, he may have watched French *caillouteurs* at their knapping benches and, exercising his soldiery eye for detail, quickly appreciated the spark-raising potential of different sorts of flint.

As newly appointed Master-General he lost little time in weeding out superfluous staff at the Tower of London and cracking down on some of the Board's long-favoured suppliers of gunflints to that arsenal. On 2nd August, 1782, the Duke presided over a Board meeting which among other business considered a petition from Thomas Lufkin, a flint supplier for "near eight years", who asked that his stock in hand be received at the Tower. To bolster his cause — he was obviously a countryman, probably from distant parts — he said he had been detained in London for three months, awaiting the Board's reply.

He received a dusty answer. The Board told him that he need not have stayed in town. Moreover, since his flints were bad, it was going to advertise to secure flints of better quality.

The Duke's concern for good flints showed again in an instruction to his dispatch clerk on 8th November that year. He called for the immediate chartering of the *Second Achilles*, the ship to be loaded forthwith with 2,000 stand of arms along with 2,000 barrels of powder and 200,000 musket flints *to be picked* (my italics), also 10,000 for carbines and 1,000 for wallpieces.

References to flints in the minutes of the Board's meetings chaired by the Surveyor-General further underline their use and importance. On 29th August, 1789, the Office of Ordnance at Upnor Castle received instructions to release 840 musket flints with 44 cwt. of ball to enable the newly embodied West Kent Regiment of Militia to carry out its training programme, field exercises and firing practices. Three months later, orders went out to supply three detachments of foot stationed at Chatham with 200 musket flints, their allocation as guards for transports about to sail conveying convicts to New South Wales.

By 1790, Thomas Lufkin had, it seemed, partially redeemed his reputation as a flint supplier. The Tower of London's Master Furbisher, Ambrose Pardoe, reported on the good quality of samples he had submitted. Then, after obtaining a quotation from Lufkin, the Board on 17th September directed him to supply 10,000 carbine flints at twelve shillings p.m. (per mille) and the same quantity of pistol flints at ten shillings p.m. Otherwise it ignored his stock in hand of 150,000 flints.

The Duke, prone to lose interest in some matters after tackling them with feverish energy, cannot be charged with growing cold on flints. When at the Surveyor-General's meeting on 6th July, 1790, an offer by William Levett of Northfleet, a one-time warrant holder to the Board, to supply flints "agreeable to a sample" was heard, it was at once decided to forward his sample to the Master-General. In his reply the Duke said that Levett's flints appeared to be "both good and bad, but if he would undertake to supply the black sort free from spots within a quarter of an inch of the sharp edge, he might send his proposals." He should be told, however, that "light coloured flints and those with spots close to the sharp edge could not be received."

A week or two earlier a momentous switch in direction had taken place in the Board's orders for gunflints. It brought East Anglia into the picture with, so far as records go, dramatic expedition. And since the Duke in person initiated this transition, he may fairly be described not just as the master stimulant but as the true godfather of Brandon's gunflint industry. Without his intervention, its renown might never have been.

At its meeting in Westminster on 16th June, 1790, the Surveyor-General and his fellow Board members took note of a letter addressed by His Grace to

Mr Philip Hayward, of Bury St Edmunds, Suffolk, directing him to deliver at the Tower "100,000 flints of the best sort", payment being twenty shillings p.m. That price must have lifted the eyebrows of old-established contractors like Thomas Lufkin, William Levett and John Burgon. The last, a London hardware merchant, had offered that selfsame month to supply the Board with "40,000 musket flints or any quantity of a superior quality" at twelve shillings p.m. He was asked to submit a sample of 1,000 gunflints.

Charles Lennox, 3rd Duke of Richmond, Master-General of the Ordnance, 1782-95, whose interest in gunflints led him to place an order in East Anglia.

What accounts for this sudden, almost open-handed and handsomely priced invitation to Philip Hayward? Mr Seymour de Lotbiniere, after turning up Hayward's name in Board of Ordnance documents, began researching into his Suffolk background and discovered that in 1793 Philip Hayward, already described as a Brandon flint manufacturer, purchased Flint Hall in the town and built cottages almost adjacent to accommodate knappers.

Hayward, a specialist, it seems, in supplying top quality black gunflints, was unlikely to earn the Duke's reprimand by sending in any with spotted or jagged firing edges. His business sense, too, was acute. Shortly after getting this contract, he asked the Board for monthly payment for flints delivered to the Tower. It decided to draw his bills twenty days after receiving the Tower's certificates as to quantities supplied.

It is not clear whether Hayward, when setting up as a gunflint manu-facturer in Brandon, moved into an established industry to furnish it with a new outlet or whether he pioneered a new craft in an immemorially flint-conscious town. One day pundits may resolve this poser. What appears unambiguous is the Board of Ordnance's recognition of and sustained faith in the spark-inducing quality of the region's unrivalled black flint.

Again, to initiate a fresh controversy, what impelled the Duke of Richmond to turn as if in a flash of inspiration to East Anglia for manu-factured flints? As Mr de Lotbiniere discovered, two miles east of Brandon the Duke's cousin, Charles Sloane, later Lord Cadogan, owned the Santon Downham estate, which can have been little better than a blowing, bleak, sandy, rabbit-swarming acreage except for plantations and water meadows beside the Little Ouse River below the Hall. Embedded inside the estate's chalk ridge rested, as for millions of years past, some of the finest black flint in Britain. Can this cousin have dropped a word in the Duke's ear? If so, had trials at the butts demonstrated the black gunflint's superiority to other sorts?

The Duke enjoyed foxhunting at Goodwood, where he entertained his sporting friends. May we not picture him, true to his restless nature and spirit of inquiry, joining his cousin at Santon Downham for a shooting party or deer hunt? Perhaps after a day's drive or a tramp across warrens accompanied by beaters, keepers and dogs, blazing off at whatever ran or flew, including bustards, the Duke and his host settled down to claret or port beside a crackling fire and discussed the behaviour of their sporting guns, and not least the activating flint.

In 1795 the Duke was deprived of his appointment as Master-General of the Ordnance. His dismissal mortified him, but his ghost, if still tempestuous, can assuredly take comfort from the vital legacy he bequeathed to British musketry through his intimate interest in gunflints.

So high stood the reputation of black flint quarried on the Santon Downham estate that Colonel Peter Hawker in his *Instructions to Young Sportsmen* (1814) prefaces his precepts about screwing flints with leather into gun cocks by stating "none are better than the most transparent of common black flints", of which a footnote says, "Great quantities (considered as good as any) come to London from Lord Cadogan's estate at Brandon."

Several theories seek to account for the discovery of this flint's consistent reaction to knapping hammers and its durability in striking sparks off steel. Flints of different grades long provided building stone for houses, cottages and walls in the region. An important Breckland industry consisted of quarrying chalk, not solely to get clunch for wall ballast but for crushing and burning to make lime. Chalk pits, sunk to depths of twenty to fifty feet, must have exposed the black flint, either as white-skinned nodules or as slabs, later known as "floorstone". The true function of Grime's Graves was still obscure, so no one at this time knew of Neolithic man's preference for the same black seam.

"Floorstone" was also pierced or dislodged whenever wells were dug in the locality. A medieval well excavated at Croxton, near Thetford, in 1979 had walls strengthened with hand-made chalk blocks which its builders presumably dug out as they sunk their shaft. When in business as a blacksmith, toolmaker and general handyman, Mr Albert Wing, aged 85 in 1980, recalled descending and cleaning out several deep wells in the Brandon area. At Lingheath Farm he found a big lump of "floorstone" lying at the bottom of the shaft. Sydney B. J. Skertchly in his gunflint memoir (1879) referred to the discovery of "floorstone" at Shaker's Lodge on Wangford Rabbit Warren, two miles south-east of Brandon, during the sinking of a well. As the hill there rises 163 feet above sea level, it is no surprise that Mr Wing should describe that well as the deepest he ever descended.

However vigorously one may discount an unbroken tradition of handling flint transmitted generation by generation from the Stone Age, logic suggests that the particular quality of this black flint stratum had been recognised for centuries because of (a) its behaviour when struck, (b) its power to activate sparks, (c) its lasting quality and (d) its attraction as a wall decoration.

At some moment in time, a Brandon man must have picked up a hammer or stone and fractured a lump of this dark, enticing flint. To his surprise, he would have noticed that the fragment which splintered off had neither spots nor impurities and that it broke freely (or, as later craftsmen expressed it, "ran well"), characteristics that proved its superiority to weathered flints or grey stones dug out nearer the surface. Then, as such realisation glimmered within, some instinct, a phoenix faith or inherited hunch, would have told him he could work effectively with it.

At the beginning of the nineteenth century, Birmingham displaced London as the nation's main centre for small arms manufacture. Colonel Miller, the Board of Ordnance's Inspector of Small Arms, appointed officers to watch its interests there. They had plenty to occupy them when on 28th March, 1804, the Board handed Birmingham a substantial contract for supplying muskets of the India pattern. To complete its order, agreements were concluded with eleven gun makers, twenty lock makers, seven bayonet makers and eleven rammer makers. Each component had a set price placed on it—16s. (80p.) for stocking and setting up, 7s. 8d. (38½p.) for the barrel, 6s. 6d. (32½p.) for lock, 2s. 6d. (12½p.) for bayonet, 8d. (3p.) for rammer and 9d. (3½p.) for lock hardening, bringing the total cost of a new musket to £1 14s. 1d. (£1.70).

At the same time, nine Brandon gunflint makers were commissioned by the Board to supply its Birmingham depot with 360,000 flints a month in the proportion of 1,000 musket flints to every fifty carbine and fifty pistol flints.

The price settled for was one guinea (£1.05) a thousand for Muskets and one pound a thousand for Carbines and Pistols. In a working year, that contract directed just under £4,500 into the pockets of these Brandon flint masters.

What would be an exhibit in the Tower of London's Armouries or a gem in any private collector's cabinet is an all-metal gunflint pattern stamped with the Board of Ordnance's cipher. Whether the Board issued such specifications for gunflint makers' guidance for each new weapon passed for sea or land service is uncertain, but one such specimen, now privately owned, emerged as a model for flints required for the Baker rifle, invented in 1801.

Of flint makers active in Brandon in the year of Trafalgar, Abraham Jacob, William Southwell, Joseph Leach, John Boggis, Roland Boggis and William Peveretts knapped niches for themselves in the town's industrial history. By 1810, several other makers swelled the roll, among them William

Part of an indenture binding a boy apprentice to Elizabeth Grief, flint master, who undertakes to teach him "the art of a gunflint maker which she now useth," 1811.   *Suffolk Record Office*

Oxley, Robert Bretnall, William Trett and Richard Money Thirkettle. All shared in Board of Ordnance contracts, and if they or their knappers gambled with guinea pieces, not all, it may be supposed, used their gains to slake dry and aching throats.

Additional evidence for the relatively late entry of Brandon in Board of Ordnance contracts may be deduced from the town's surviving assortment of apprentice indentures. Some forty, preserved by the Suffolk Record Office at Bury St Edmunds, vary in date from early in the eighteenth century to the first quarter of the nineteenth century. Of these, two only relate to gunflint apprenticeships.

It might be argued that such a craft in its early phase did not merit apprenticeship status. But that seems a fruitless line to pursue since indentures sealed in Brandon related not only to the art and mystery of a cordwainer and the trade and occupation of a barber or perriwig maker but to such very ordinary trades as the mystery and business of a sheepherd (sic), the art of ploughing and sowing and all things belonging to husbandry (an indenture dated 1745) and most frequently to the trade and occupation of a waterman. Nearly all such jobs demanded less skill and practice than a flintmaker needed for all-round competence in his craft.

Of the two gunflint indentures, the earlier concerns William Clark, "a poor child of Brandon", who on 30th January, 1804, was apprenticed to his namesake William Clark Junior, a gunflint manufacturer in the town, and pledged "to learn the art and mystery of his master's craft until he reach 21." The churchwardens and vestry overseer compounded this apprenticeship by a payment of ten pounds. No wage for the boy was mentioned, but the flint master agreed to provide him throughout his apprentice years with "sufficient meat, drink, apparel, lodging, washing and other things for an apprentice" and guaranteed that he would not be a charge on the parish or its parishioners.

The second indenture is a contract between Elizabeth Grief, gunflint maker of Brandon, and George Maidens. An "infant" of eleven, he was bound to her on 12th April, 1813, for seven years. This may be the first record of a woman flint master, possibly carrying on her late husband's business, but breaking into a dusty, health-sapping male preserve. The parish elders sealed this indenture, and paid Elizabeth Grief £8 for contracting "to teach and instruct or cause to be taught and instructed" the boy Maidens "in the art of a gunflint maker which she now useth."

In lieu of meat, drink, lodging and other necessities during his term, he received four shillings (20p.) a week for the first year of his apprenticeship, a wage increased by a shilling (5p.) a week per year until his contract expired. In return, paragon-like behaviour was expected of him. He had to serve his mistress faithfully, keep her secrets, cause no damage to her property and tell her if he saw it done by others. Furthermore, as the age's legal jargon insisted, "he shall neither buy nor sell without the said Mistress's licence. Taverns, Inns or Alehouses he shall not haunt. At Cards Dice Tables or any other unlawful Game he shall not play, nor from the Service of his said Mistress Day or Night absent himself but in all things as an honest and faithful Apprentice shall and will demean himself towards his said Mistress and all her's during the said term."

Of Brandon's knapping families the most conspicuous, according to historical records, is the Snare family, five generations of which managed flint shops in the town. It is revealing, however, to find that in 1746 Robert Snare,

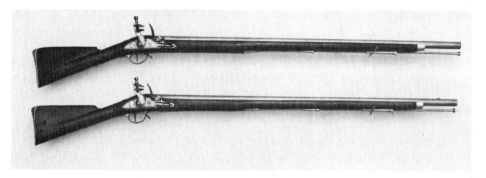

India pattern muskets as used by Wellington's "squares." *The Armouries, HM Tower of London. Crown copyright, reproduced with permission of the Controller of HMSO.*

described as a child of Brandon, was apprenticed to Charles Burres, a blacksmith of Emswell Thorn, possibly located in Elmswell. Had the Snares already established themselves as flint masters, such an apprenticeship would be unlikely. The indenture bound Robert until he attained "his full age of 24 years", his master providing him with "double apparel of all sorts, good and new (that is to say) a good new suit for the Holy Days and another for the Working Days."

While this young Snare was occupied shoeing horses, breaking up metals, repairing or manufacturing farm implements, his eye would be sharpened and hand steadied in sizing up and shaping materials. The craft sense acquired at the forge might materially benefit his children and grandchildren once they began hammering flint instead of iron.

Some legal matters reflect Brandon's management of its knapping industry. In March, 1811, the parish's churchwardens sought the advice of Frederick Const, counsel at the Temple, to determine the parish's obligations under the terms of agreements between flint masters and two men who were then seeking poor relief. Philip Hayward again steps into the picture. For by an agreement signed and countersigned on 21st April, 1800, Joseph Heigham of Thetford, then about twenty years old, undertook to work for Hayward, a gunflint maker of Brandon, his executors or administrators, for a term of seven years and "not make less than 2,000 Common or 1,500 Seconds gunflints every day." It was agreed that during his seven years Heigham should not work for anyone else or for his own benefit without Hayward's consent, nor disclose his business and — this is an extraordinary contractual clause — "not to take advantage of his agreement in case the wages or any part thereof shall happen to be one month in arrears." In brief, cash withheld — no complaints!

On his side, Hayward contracted to pay Heigham wages of ten shillings a week throughout the seven years, plus "the usual journeyman's wages" for all gunflints made over the quantity specified. Heigham lodged in Brandon. He had to find basic necessities for himself and by 1811 had become a pauper. In appealing for relief, he said that Hayward allowed him half a crown (12½p.) a week as living money, but felt aggrieved because after he had completed part of his term, his master left Brandon for a considerable period and on returning forced him to work out his full seven years. In counsel's opinion, such an agreement could not be construed as an apprenticeship indenture. It fell into the category of contracts with hired servants, by which a servant had settlement rights in whichever parish he slept with his master's consent. So this ruling established Joseph Heigham, formerly of Thetford, as a legal settler in Brandon.

Incorrect drafting, rather than any attempt at exploitation, marred the contract between Robert Judd, a Weeting boy, and Richard Rissbrook, a gunflint maker of Brandon. With his father's consent, young Robert undertook to serve seven years at the trade, receiving 4s. (20p.) a week for the first year, 5s. (25p.) a week for the second year and with corresponding rises annually to his final year. These wages were deemed to be in lieu of meat, drink, lodging, washing and so forth, the usual provisions made by masters for their apprentices. The boy Judd continued to live with his father at Weeting. It was customary for flint masters who accepted apprentices or engaged boys at apprentice rates to teach them their craft, whatever was or was not written into an agreement, this particular contract omitting any mention of an undertaking by Rissbrook to instruct the boy in gunflint manufacture. That assuredly was taken for granted. As counsel pointed out, a contract's defects could not be remedied by an undertaking between the parties. So, through an oversight, through somebody's carelessness, what seemed clearly intended as an apprenticeship indenture was legally no more than a hiring contract. Under its terms, Robert Judd rated as a legal settler in Weeting and a charge, therefore, on that parish.

At the outset of the Napoleonic Wars, gunflints were manufactured at Lewisham, Maidstone, Purfleet, Greenhithe and Northfleet, at Beer Head,

Devon, and King Manor, Clarendon, near Salisbury. As the conflict dragged on, with the nation's fleet expanding under threat of invasion and the Board of Ordnance extending and re-equipping its coastal fortifications, Brandon's black flints advanced swiftly in reputation and demand. Rival manufactories lost government orders and either concentrated on building flints or ceased business. Before the French Emperor's overthrow, the Suffolk town probably had the gunflint field to itself.

So far as Brandon is concerned, the industry's red letter day dawned on Friday, 19th February, 1813, when at a meeting of the Board of Ordnance in Pall Mall, chaired by the Lieutenant-General with the Surveyor-General also present, the following Brandon flint masters were invited to enter into an agreement to supply flints for one year from 1st March. The monthly quota assigned to individual makers, as recorded in the Board's minutes, was:

W. Clarke to supply	90,000	musquet flints, and not to exceed							135,000
R. Curry	,,	90,000	,,	,,	,,	,, ,,	,,	135,000
J. Wharf	,,	60,000	,,	,,	,,	,, ,,	,,	90,000
J. Snare and Son	,,	100,000	,,	,,	,,	,, ,,	,,	156,000
J. Utting	,,	90,000	,,	,,	,,	,, ,,	,,	135,000
W. Wood	,,	90,000	,,	,,	,,	,, ,,	,,	135,000
A. Grief	,,	80,000	,,	,,	,,	,, ,,	,,	120,000
W. Rissbrook	,,	100,000	,,	,,	,,	,, ,,	,,	140,000

The price of musket flints was fixed at one guinea (£1.05) per mille and that of carbine and pistol flints at nineteen shillings (95p.) p.m. No grey flints were to be received. With every 8,000 flints, the contractors were to supply 1,000 carbine flints and 400 large pistol flints. No small pistol flints were required. The contractors had to bear carriage costs to the Tower and "defray the expense of viewing all such rejected flints as shall exceed one eighth part of the whole number delivered for viewing at the rate of 8d. per thousand, the amount thereof to be deducted from their bills quarterly." The eight men so scheduled were established contractors.

About the same time the Board offered contracts at identical rates but with conditions more explicitly stated to six new men. Their names and the quantities particularised were as follows:

Josiah Curzon to supply	60,000	musquet flints, and not to exceed							80,000
Thomas Longworth	60,000	,,	,,	,,	,, ,,	,,	80,000
William Southwill (sic)	60,000	,,	,,	,,	,, ,,	,,	80,000
Michael Phillips	60,000	,,	,,	,,	,, ,,	,,	80,000
Abraham Jacob	60,000	,,	,,	,,	,, ,,	,,	80,000
Richard Rissbrook Jnr	60,000	,,	,,	,,	,, ,,	,,	80,000

Upon their agreeing to the Board's terms, they were advised that no grey coarse flints were acceptable nor any white heeled ones. Also, at its meeting on 3rd March, the Board decreed that no contractor be allowed to employ men of another contractor to fulfil his order, and moreover "the contractors are to expressly understand that nothing but black flints for muskets, carbines and pistols of the best quality are to be sent to the Tower, each sort separated from the other." The agreement as before covered one year from 1st March.

So altogether fourteen Brandon flint masters were called on in a national emergency to supply a monthly quota of 1,060,000 musket flints, their total

The lock of an India pattern musket. *The Armouries, HM Tower of London.*
Crown copyright, reproduced with permission of the Controller of HMSO.

production restricted to 1,526,000 flints a month. At its lowest valuation, but without deductions lost through rejections, this contract was worth £13,167 in a year, and at its highest £18,955. It meant full employment for about 160 knappers and stone diggers. By the standards of 1813, it was a magnificent, indeed astronomically rich, order for splitting among what the Board termed artificers in a township of little more than 1,300 people.

Flints, however excellent in quality, would not have gained an ascendancy in officialdom's reckoning unless well knapped. Here it seems that Brandon's manufacturers were indebted to a prisoner of war from the enemy country. This provokes an intriguing reflection. For if it was a Frenchman who passed on knowledge of flint craft learned in his native land, then he contributed both to the result of Waterloo and to Europe's destiny emerging from that battle.

The French in the heyday of their flintlock-serviced armies had about 800 people engaged in gunflint manufacture. The department of Loire et Cher contained rich deposits of flint in its chalk beds, and *caillouteurs* chipped away at centres such as Meusnes, Pouilly, Ange, Noyers and Couffy. A commune in Indre called Lye also had its mines and flint makers and Citizen Dolomieu, an early authority on the French craft, told of an emigré from Meusnes, possibly an escapee from feudal bondage there, who set up his shop and knapped for thirty years at La Roche Guyon, a village overlooking the Seine where in a war of more recent memory Rommel set up his headquarters as he endeavoured to repel the Allied invasion.

I went there in August, 1944, after the Normandy battle and entered the cavern tunnelled in the chalk rock beside the chateau of the La Rochefoucauld family, from which the German supremo organised his counter attacks. The cliff top overhead was pitted with neatly dug slit trenches, some protected by barbed wire entanglements. A smashed radio station, discarded equipment, ammunition and grenades, some attached to trip wires, scarred the scene, so quiet on a summer's day. As I poked around, I never guessed that beneath me lay a flint seam whose exploitation had affinity with Brandon's industry.

With production so widespread and intensive, it would have been odd had the French kept their gunflint manufacturing processes to themselves. The Scottish geologist, Dr James Mitchell, on his visit to Brandon in the 1830s, heard from Jeremiah Simmonds that it was his grandfather, James Woodyer,

A French caillouteur and his wife. The husband flakes with a pointed hammer while his wife uses a roulette, a disc-headed hammer, to knap his flakes against a chisel-like projection.

Musée Pierre à Fusil, France

who had introduced the pointed French flaking hammer to England. Woodyer, who lived at Kingston, between Maidstone and London, had in 1837 been dead for more than fifty years. So possibly the French introduction took root in Kent some years before Brandon adopted it.

However, there are other claimants or, it would be fairer to say, individuals championing them. An oral tradition seized on by Sydney Rogerson in the 1920's attributed the transition in manufacturing style to a French POW named Fruer. Captured during the Napoleonic Wars and put to forced labour in Brandon, he allegedly denigrated the round-headed hammers

Diagram of a gunflint, double-backed or "platform" style, knapped from a long flake by French-type hammer.

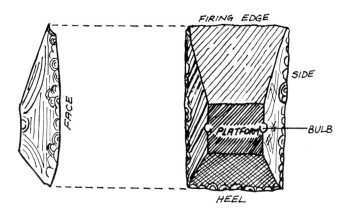

he saw knappers using in their shops for striking flakes. Such bash-and-hope methods outraged his craft sense. So he demonstrated how much finer flakes, longer, double or single backed with sharp flanges, could be struck with a point-headed hammer. This Fruer, like POW's in bloodier wars, grew attached to the place of his captivity, married a local girl, settled in Brandon and anglicised his name to Frewer. A man with this name had a small flint mining and knapping business outside Norwich in the 1870's.

During that decade another individual, of whom it is hard to say whether he was real or a figment of the imagination, entered the source list, a French POW referred to as Pero. The energetic, persistently inquisitive Sydney Skertchly picked up his name when talking to an aged knapper in Brandon, but the knapper was not speaking from personal acquaintance, only passing on what his grandfather had told him. Skertchly, prone in the eyes of some critics to dwell too readily on ancient links, supposed that Pero had arrived in Brandon during Marlborough's campaigns.

Whichever explanation is true, the French mode of flake production applied to Brandon's black flint gave the town what was for long an unassailable status as the major gunflint production centre in Britain, if not in the world.

CHAPTER SIX

Repercussions after Waterloo

WHILE Waterloo brought a famous victory and terminated Napoleon's grand designs, the flint masters of Brandon had mixed feelings about the war's end. For some it foreshadowed disaster. The Board of Ordnance, without doubt since 1660 the heaviest buyer of British gunflints, reverted to a policy of wait and see. Contracts were not renewed. Short of another national emergency, the Board appeared satisfied that its stocks of gunflints at the Tower and at other home and overseas depots were adequate for the time being.

Brandon's industry, its fortunes swollen by the recent boom, hardly knew which way to turn. The hardest-headed masters kept going, but those neither so energetic nor so uncompromising were soon in trouble. Paradoxically, both sorts of employers, the tough no less than the moderate, contributed by their treatment of knappers and stone diggers to discontent, suffering and poverty, ills which the town had to alleviate by its own limited administration and resource. That area of Lingheath constituting the Poor's Allotment, the legacy of the Enclosure Act, might be thought of as a buffer against destitution. But it was no social security bank and, despite its flint wealth, far from an equitable recompense for the loss of common rights.

Even before the bonanza, Church and parish joined forces in an effort to promote the best use of its flint to counter unemployment. A scheme agreed between the Vestry, which represented St Peter's Church, and the parish on 11th January, 1813, allowed Brandon's poor to raise stone on Lingheath, the flint masters hiring their labour at "3s. 9d. a load in consideration of building stone."

Within a month or two the flint masters, not entirely happy about their payments for estimated loads, asked the Vestry to erect a weighing machine on the heath. The Vestry responded after its meeting on 11th April by informing these contractors that a weighing machine could be erected, but only at their expense. Weighing loads involved extra labour, probably unrewarded, since there was no alternative to placing flints on the machine before loading them into carts or wagons for transport to the knapping shops. Not long afterwards the Vestry thought the flint masters were getting too good a bargain. So, on 2nd August, it increased charges for building stone dug from the heath to 4s. (20p.) a load. On its part, the parish agreed to bear the cost of levelling pits.

The depression caused by the end of the war not only meant extra mouths to feed as soldiers returned from the battlefields and ships lay up and crews paid off, but a sudden inflation in food prices aggravated the struggles of those subsisting on the breadline. Parish relief offered little more than a charitable pittance. So, through one cause and another, Brandon fell under the shadow of the agrarian riots that bedevilled East Anglia. Initially, the town's aggrieved citizens vented their wrath against Mr Norman, the Weeting miller, whom they regarded as responsible for raising flour prices and denying them bread. But their anger was also directed against the Brandon butcher, Thomas Willett, reviled by some as another infamous profiteer, and against the proprietor of the *White Hart Inn* in High Street. Without bread, meat or beer, life was insupportable.

The rioting began on 16th May, 1816, and at first was relatively mild. But a day or two later discontent hotted up as troublemakers from Bury St Edmunds, Thetford and farther afield streamed into the town, some armed with iron-spiked sticks; one with a flintlock. Helen Dyer, a well-built, comely young woman, but with no pretensions to being a ringleader, displayed a banner daubed with the slogan "Bread or Blood in Brandon this Day". She hoisted it high like a battle standard in the Market Square. The crowd, larger and more ill-tempered, took up the cry, yelling for a reduction in flour prices. If not, their threat would be made reality.

The local constables could not cope. Magistrates reacted in alarm and fear. Although the Riot Act was read two or three times, the crowd refused to be placated until its demands were met. Better grant concessions, nervous

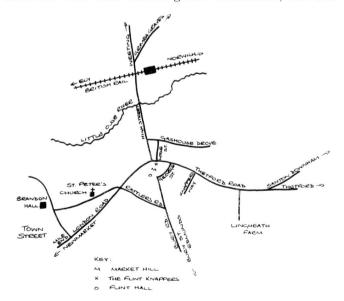

A plan of Brandon showing the church's situation in relation to the town centre, at the meeting place of the main roads, and Town Street, for generations almost a separate community.

KEY:
M MARKET HILL
X THE FLINT KNAPPERS
O FLINT HALL

authority seem to say, than risk widespread plunder or murder. The men had a free distribution of beer on the *Ram Inn* meadow. But even so, their tempers were not wholly cooled, nor their thirst quenched. Some rioting followed, and before the mob dispersed a disorderly faction had raided and demolished with savage ferocity the shop and home of Willett, the butcher.

Though food suppliers bore the brunt of the town's odium, some of its misfortune could be laid legitimately at the door of the flint masters whose piecework rates, exacting in the extreme, cut their employees' earnings to just a shade above pauper level. In fairness, though, these contractors were in turn at the mercy of merchants as tough-minded as themselves, their overriding aim being to buy stocks of gunflints at the cheapest possible rates for export or for sale to gunsmiths serving the sporting fraternity.

Knappers and stone diggers might starve, but the locality's black flint preserved its reputation untarnished. It was never disparaged. On the contrary, W. H. Scott, proffering advice on powder and shot in his *Field Sports*, first published in 1818, remarked: "Transparent, black Norfolk or Brandon flints, are among the best, or those of a hard white stone, and of such the Gunner should provide himself with a good store; for to be sparing of flints is to be accessory to his own loss of time and vexation." Despite this observation, later, in the same volume, he warns his readers against hard white flint stone as "it requires too great a force in the Cock and is extremely injurious to the Hammer."

St Peter's Church, Brandon, whose Vestry once ran the town's flint knapping business.

Peter Burrin

By 1801 Brandon's population stood at 1,148, rising to 1,360 in 1811, by which time, according to Frederic Schoberl, there were about 201 houses in the town. The advance in numbers, if described as steady, was restrained more by heavy child mortality than by bread riots or food shortages. At the 1821 census the town's population was 1,770, made up of 353 families, of whom 62 had no regular work. Trade and manufacture, which included flint making, supported 137 families; 20 depended on agriculture, 117 on heavy labour, and 17, though not out of work, did not state their occupation. There were 380 girls and 390 boys under fifteen.

Because of mounting hardship and the disarray into which the industry had fallen, on 23rd November, 1821, the Vestry of St Peter's Church took the unprecedented step of entering the gunflint trade, in effect setting up business as a contemporary munitions manufacturer. It was an extraordinary but laudable example of the Church militant in action. On that day, its representatives concluded an agreement with seven flint masters in the town "for the manufacture of flints for the said Vestry and no other person or persons at the current prices of wages." Of the seven contractors, five appended their signatures by a mark. The Vestry appointed an overseer to watch over this consortium.

Its creation, by any standards a bold stroke of initiative, promised a more rational approach to an industry rocked back on its heels as perhaps never before. In France, following the Napoleonic débâcle, huge stocks of gunflints built up over the war years no longer had military significance. If not secretly preserved for export, quantities were crushed by the resourceful French into pathways, and even chateaux used supplies to metal their carriageways. It was not for Brandon to emulate that French pattern.

Further evidence of disorientation appeared when, also in 1821, one master discharged eight knappers and, during the same month, 18 labourers, most of them stone diggers, were thrown out of work. All applied for parish relief. And at least one flint master, John Rissbrook, fared worse, being unable to meet his liabilities. The magistrates committed him to Bury gaol where he languished until ordered to appear at the Quarter Sessions on 20th June, 1821, for examination as an insolvent debtor.

The plight of out-of-work flint knappers provoked sententious comment. Having appraised Lingheath as an asset for relieving poverty, one custodian of public virtue, or a mere minute taker, blandly observed: "Employment to the labouring poor appears to us a paramount object since it not only ensures an amendment to their moral habits but provides for them work to enable them to support themselves and their families."

Towards the end of that abysmal year the parish went to the expense of adding flint shops to its workhouse. This introduction took some of the sting out of the misery of unemployment for, even if forced to exist on minimal

Carting barrels of gunflints packed for export. Robert W. "Bill" Basham, designer of the flint necklace and alphabet illustrated on pages 110 and 113, is the tall man second from right.
Seymour de Lotbiniere collection

rations, the knapper could maintain his craft skills. Its advantages, too, appealed to less scrupulous masters who paid their men inadequate wages and then expected the parish to make up the sum necessary for their subsistence. "Now," a skinflint employer might say to a hapless knapper, "if you don't like what you're getting here, you can carry on — in the workhouse."

To its credit the Vestry set about its new interests speedily in a businesslike manner. It continued selling gunflints by the thousand, retaining the French abbreviation m. for mille. In correspondence with the Birmingham firm of S. Rawlins & Co, its representative in April, 1822, summarised the Vestry's stock in hand as 44 m. Fine Singles and 17 m. Second Singles. The Birmingham firm replied by asking for the lowest prices for delivery of both sorts of flints to Mr Bird's warehouse at the *Bell Inn* in Wood Street, Cheapside, London.

Writing again in June to the Gentlemen of the Select Vestry, Brandon, S. Rawlins & Co. complained about unfair competition; another person, assumed to be the agent of a London house, was selling flints in Birmingham. Although the quantities sold were trifling, it was felt that such competition kept prices down. "We are confident," the firm wrote, "that it cannot answer for more than one warehouse to sell flints in Birmingham to enable them to

70

pay rent and expenses, and those who are now trying will soon find their error."

For its own good the Select Vestry was advised to "engage the whole of the mines" and thus by controlling supplies of raw flint prevent small flint masters from manufacturing and selling flints to dealers wherever found. Given a monopoly, so the Birmingham argument ran, the Vestry could fix prices on a scale that guaranteed the industry's workers a decent livelihood — admirable sentiments from a firm primarily interested in the cheapest possible quotations.

Its advice did not end there. For after admitting that prices for gunflints were already too low, and would be further reduced if the Vestry resorted to sales by auction, S. Rawlins & Co. candidly stated that it held flints valued at £1,300 and, with its sights fixed on future prosperity, asked the Vestry to find as much alternative labour as possible for knappers and diggers until stocks built up by all dealers "might be a little exhausted."

The Vestry held to its aim of keeping knappers active. A London agent was appointed with his headquarters in Lincoln Chambers, and plans were made to transfer gunflint stocks from Bishopsgate, where they were inadequately stored, to a warehouse in Lincoln's Inn Fields close to his office. Did St Peter's congregation sit up with a jerk, I wonder, when this item of flint business drafted by William Mortlock, the Vestry clerk, was read out at morning service on Sunday, 27th October, 1822?

> "Notice is hereby given that a Select Vestry will be held at the usual time and place on Wednesday next to receive tenders for conveying the flints to London and determining the sorts and quantity immediately to be sent, also to adopt means for the better regulating of the poor in digging and manufacture. Further notice is given that Mr Thomas Mortlock (overseer) is granted a rate of one and sixpence in the pound which is allowed and signed by the magistrates."

When submitting his tender James Smith, of Wangford, forwarded an open letter from J. Holdom of the *Vine Inn*, in which Holdom undertook to cart flints from Brandon to Lincoln's Inn Fields at five shillings (25p.) per cwt. and transfer those stacked in Bishopsgate to that warehouse at the same rate. Holdom's artless faith in human kind said little for his management of a village pub. For Smith, who was not born yesterday, offered to cart flints from Brandon to London for four shillings (20p.) per cwt. and, having undercut his ingenuous neighbour, added, "I shall be much obliged by the preference."

The contract, however, went to Thomas Archer, a carrier from Barton Place, Mildenhall. His price was no more than 2s. 6d. (12½p.) per cwt. for lifting flints from Brandon to London and a mere sixpence (2½p.) per cwt. to transfer stocks from Bishopsgate to Lincoln's Inn Fields. There was, however, a significant proviso. Their fortunes clipped by loss of orders, Brandon's flint masters had, it seemed, acquired a poor reputation in the locality for paying their bills. Archer insisted that he regarded the officers of the Vestry as his customers and relied on their payment for his carriage of flints as soon as he had delivered their orders, but "if the manufacturers of the flints are themselves to pay the carriage, I should beg to decline having anything to do with them."

Under the chairmanship of James Miller, the committee of the Select Vestry undertook the management of Brandon's entire gunflint trade. Control of the parish workhouse manufactory was not the smallest of its responsibilities. This, it agreed, must provide employment for all out-of-work flint knappers and diggers in the parish. Meeting on Christmas Eve, 1822, the committee drafted rules regulating the price of flints quarried and carted from Lingheath. Under their provisions, Brandon's flint masters could buy flint stones, quality unspecified, at seventeen shillings (85p.) a load on delivery to their works. But for anyone whose knapping shop was in Town Street, three quarters of a mile west of the High Street, an extra sixpence ($2\frac{1}{2}$p.) a load was chargeable. Each master must pay the carter before he dropped a stone in their yards. If he could not produce the cash, the carter was instructed to turn his horse about and drop the load at the workhouse. Building stone could be bought at the heath at five shillings (25p.) a wagonload and three shillings (15p.) a cartload. But again, as a counter to bilkers, the committee authorised its overseer or watchdog to collect all such dues as the stones were being loaded.

By the end of 1822, despite the Birmingham firm's plea for restraints on production and the depletion of existing stocks, a total of 1,218,535 gunflints sat in barrels and kegs on the floors of warehouses in Brandon and London. Earlier a Vestry resolution had called for the building of a double cottage on Lingheath to accommodate "two mechanics of approved character well versed in the trade." The committee hoped that Lingheath's Trustees would finance such an undertaking and equip the cottages with flint workshops and a warehouse. The innovation would in its view not simply improve the estate belonging to the poor of Brandon but "be a resource in further years for providing labour for that description of poor who being bred to the trade are unfitted for agricultural work." Such a proposal indicated advanced long-term thinking, and showed confidence in the craft's continuity in spite of current difficulties.

Mining flints afforded no better livelihood than knapping. It was just as precarious and ill-paid, the one advantage recognised and appreciated being a greater sense of personal freedom as the miner wielded his single-pronged pick in a chalk hole by himself rather than toiling with hammers in a hot dusty shed with his fellows. No more than a fractional variation in earnings, the difference of a shilling or two, marked a flint miner's weekly takings from 1820 to 1936.

The Ashley family cannot be paralleled for its record among the town's stone diggers on Lingheath. Arthur "Pony" Ashley deserves a place in industrial history as the last to burrow full-time down to its flint beds. The family's earnings throughout successive generations confirm an almost unchanging wages structure. For a week's work spent sinking a pit, May 4-10, 1821, William Ashley earned seven shillings (35p.); the following week he raised a load, lifting his income to eight shillings (40p.). On 20th November,

Arthur "Pony" Ashley peers up from the entrance to one of his shafts at Lingheath. *Herbert Field collection*

in return for a week's labour, during which he mined three-quarters of a load, he pocketed nine shillings (45p.). The going rate for excavating a full wagonload then stood at twelve shillings (60p.).

In 1824 rewards were less attractive. On 4th June that year William Ashley earned ten shillings (50p.) for six days' work, during which he raised one load priced at seven shillings (35p.), the parish making up the deficiency. On 25th June four days' work resulting in half a load of flint brought him 3s. 6d. (17½p.); the parish with a contribution of four shillings (20p.) more than doubled his income for that week. By this time, three children and a wife depended on him. A steady, strong and experienced miner, between 4th June and 9th July he raised 3½ loads of flint for which he was paid 24s 6d. (£1.22½), and with poor relief added, his return for 26 days' work was £2 2s. 9d. (£2.14).

If ever anyone penned an unsolicited testimonial to back bending toil of this description it was Thomas Morgan. Writing from London on 20th March, 1823, about the care of his illegitimate child left in Brandon, he said: "I hope it will never be beholding to my parish for support but if it did, it has got a good one which is St Saviour Boro (Southwark). I can provide for it, not with slaving for eight shillings per week as the poor fellows are forced to do in your parish (Brandon) for I can work easy and earn that in a day."

Besides facing the difficulties of opening up fair markets for the town's gunflints, the Select Vestry fought doggedly against depression and complacency. It dealt dispassionately with on-the-spot problems and tried, so far as was within its power, to protect the industry's workers and their interests. This concern may sometimes have conflicted with compassion. A minute, recorded on 11th April, 1823, recommends that a labourer be indicted for stealing stone from the heath.

Irregularity of orders remained a prime bugbear. Large stocks accumulating without a ready outlet locked up money that was badly needed to support the workforce. Lack of initiative at the top end of the business, failure perhaps of the Vestry's London agent to establish new markets or develop existing contacts, may have accounted for the gunflint equivalent of bottlenecks, large stocks of flints piling up in vain pursuit of purchasers. In what appeared a determined effort to get things moving and clear stocks, William Mortlock, the Vestry Clerk, announced on 4th June, 1824:

> Notice is hereby given that tenders will be received at the Vestry Room on Friday 18th day of June instant at the hour of 11 o'clock in the forenoon for such gunflints belonging to the parish as are now in London at per thousand and as specified below: viz

Second Single	33,500
Common Musket	12,250
Common Gun	19,550
Fine and Superfine Single	122,750
Fine and Superfine Double	79,200

> (More or less to be delivered in London)

There was no stampede of would-be buyers, nor any spirited competition for the different sorts. Instead, one firm of merchants and flint makers, John Burgon and Son, of London and Brandon, which was bent on dominating the market for British gunflints, bought the entire stock. On 26th June, it acknowledged the receipt of 32 casks from "Officers of the Parish of Brandon containing 269,000 gunflints."

Apart from facing a merchant monopoly, the industry was overshadowed by a more formidable rival, the invention of percussion firing largely as the result of the researches of a Scottish pastor, Alexander John Forsyth, minister of Belhevie in Aberdeenshire. Much interested in chemistry, as well as being an active sportsman, as early as April, 1807, he took out a patent (No 3032) for "An advantageous Method of Discharging or Giving Fire to Artillery and all other Firearms, Mines, Chambers, Cavities and Places in which Gunpowder or other combustible Matter is or may be put for the Purpose of Explosion". By experimenting with fulminate compounds, he developed the "scent bottle" lock, which contained sufficient detonating powder for 20-25 fires. Many improvements and adaptations ensued as fresh minds developed the idea and evolved first the thimble-shaped copper percussion cap and finally the self-contained cartridge.

By 1820, if not earlier, far-sighted men saw that the new trend would render flintlocks obsolete. Percussion firing cut out the time lag, eliminated

Knapping, quartering and flaking hammers, with gunflints and flakes.
James English collection

the preliminary tell-tale puff of smoke from the flash pan, increased a weapon's rate of fire, and improved handling convenience and all-weather efficiency. For all that, military forces were surprisingly slow to recognise its advantages. France led the way. Britain, after extensive trials by individual regiments (experiments in some cases were abortive) followed in 1838, and America a year or two later. It was the old story of authorities hesitant to alter existing practices, scrap proven weapons, and face the cost of manufacturing new ones and the necessity of rewriting their training manuals.

Inventions in another field, which may be likened to a fresh body blow, also threatened to pulverise the more domestic part of Brandon's flint industry, the manufacture of large "strike-a-light" flints. In 1827, John Walker, a Stockton-on-Tees chemist, brought out his "friction lights", after which in the early thirties "lucifer matches" appeared. These were followed by the "strike anywhere" or safety match, which firms began to manufacture by the billion, and ultimately the billion million.

The strike-a-light must soon have appeared like the gunflint, a doomed commodity.

CHAPTER SEVEN

Territorial Markets lap the World

THE industry battled on as if unaware of inventions likely to crush it. In some cases, flint masters buttressed their craft by subsidiary trades such as innkeeping, farming or limeburning. With loss of Board of Ordnance contracts, new outlets were vital. The East India Company, for long both a manufacturer and a purchaser of Brandon gunflints, showed the way. As British merchantile enterprise, galvanised by the industrial revolution at home, ventured into remote ports and havens, so markets, many hitherto undreamed of, opened up for gunflints and strike-a-lights.

Retrospectively, to posit a diverting thought, a Stone Age craft ingeniously modernised entered now into the service of surviving Stone Age peoples. For traders, colonists and settlers brought with them the white man's weapons, many obsolete or obsolescent, but novel indeed to native populations and fanatically coveted, as if magically endowed, by their chiefs. As civilisation (Western standard) extended its frontiers, accompanied by disease, greed, crime and genocide as well as benefits, Birmingham-crafted flintlocks impinged on territories where for centuries past tribes had hunted and fought with clubs and spears, bows and arrows or, like the Dyaks of Borneo, blowpipes and poisoned darts.

Knapping floors in desolate country used by aborigines in Australia, in New South Wales as well as in the north, reveal the continuity of ageless practices. Archaeologists comment on the wastefulness of their methods. For the near-naked flaker, sitting on his stony or rock-strewn floor, lifts his stone hammer tirelessly and sometimes strikes off 300-400 flakes before he finds one that satisfies him as a knife.

The savage, often a splendid physical specimen, settled in some jungle fastness or remote valley or on some Pacific Island, knew nothing of powder and shot except from the receiving end. His credulity and dread of or child-like curiosity about new weapons was at times callously exploited. During the period 1804-1815, Birmingham craftsmen turned out 1,827,889 muskets and pistols for the Board of Ordnance. Before and after this output, some gunmakers specialised in manufacturing cheap flintlocks for export. Discarded service weapons, broken or obsolete, were also bought and converted, cheaply. Freelance traders, not particular about the quality or use of their wares, off-loaded these goods in tropical and other territories where few questions were asked.

Who worried whether barter-designed muskets served invidious ends? In the West Indies, buccaneers lived by their flintlocks so successfully that one type of trading gun, *fusil boucanier*, handsomely fitted with brass mount, red stock and long barrel, carried their name and was bloodily involved in their piracies. In Africa, especially on the Guinea Coast, traders profited in human cargo by selling "male" and "female" flintlocks, which were guns of cheap manufacture, long barrelled, unreliable and often a danger to their users, in return for which a chief handed over a healthy male or female slave.

At Queen Victoria's accession, Brandon's industry engaged seventy or eighty knappers and stone diggers. And, although the Army and Navy were about to reject flintlocks in favour of percussion firing arms, the industry looked forward to some resurgence, a new burst of prosperity. The Brandon Gunflint Company was formed in December, 1837, to consolidate the industry, resist monopolistic pressures, and place it on a go-ahead business footing. Prospects looked fine, on paper. A leaflet that invited shares in the new company declared:

> The advantages which present themselves are such as scarcely to be met with in any other undertaking, and renders the investment so secure as to hold out the strongest inducement to persons desirous of increasing their incomes without risk to embark in the undertaking.
>
> Brandon has always been and must continue the only place from which

A Stone Age craft in the twentieth century—aborigines chipping flakes on a rocky "floor" in New South Wales. *The Australian Museum, Sydney*

gunflints can be supplied, there not being in the kingdom any ground known from which the Stone can be obtained of the like quality and quantity to that in Brandon and the immediate neighbourhood.

During the late long and sanguinary war, all the Government contracts were executed at Brandon, and very considerable sums of money realised there. The East India Company and most foreign powers are now regularly supplied with gunflints from Brandon, and with a well-managed capital, like that proposed to be raised, and with activity in the managements of the affairs of the company, a wide field presents itself for increasing the trade to a very considerable extent.

This enterprise cobbled together the town's flint masters. But could they, obstinate, tight-fisted and independent men, in some instances rough and illiterate, unite their resources constructively? Would a cohesive, hard-bargaining, firmly controlled organisation emerge to justify such grandiose claims? The new company, aiming at a working capital of £5,000, issued 138 shares at £25 a share. Its largest shareholder, Benjamin Murrell Shepperson, described as a gentleman, bought eight shares. Three applicants each invested £100. Of the first 45 names in the shareholding list, three registered their signatures by a mark, two of them being flint masters.

Fourteen Brandon gunflint manufacturers bought shares. Their names in alphabetical order were:

William Carter	William Peverett
Robert Clark	John Rissbrook
James Claxton	John Snare
Josiah Curson	John Snare the Younger
Edward Francis	Ambrose Strickland
Michael King	Thomas Teller
William Oldby	William Trett

Of this muster, Messrs Clark, Curson and Peverett joined the company's board.

John Angerstein, a Brandon benefactor, lived then at Weeting Hall. Though not as famous as John Julius of that name, a wealthy Russian emigre (d. 1823) for the purchase of whose 38 paintings, nearly all masterpieces, the House of Commons voted £60,000 in 1824 (this collection formed the nucleus of the National Gallery), he was nevertheless a man of influence and discernment. Either he or a member of his staff spread the news that investment in the gunflint company would earn fat dividends. Among the original shareholders we find Mary Wright, his housekeeper, David Woodyer, his butler, Lionel Smith, his under-butler, James Brownlee, his gardener, Elizabeth Newell, his dairymaid, and Elizabeth Miles, lady's maid to Miss Angerstein. Possibly Angerstein himself selected these members of his staff as especially deserving because of devoted service and presented each with a £25 share. Few dairymaids in an era of underpaid labour had £25 in cash stacked away, and still fewer can have had an inclination to speculate with hardearned savings. One will never know, either, what prompted Margaret Halliday, barmaid to Richard Cook, an innkeeper at Mundford, to invest in a share. Surprisingly, in a squire-ruled hierarchy, no prejudice existed against enlisting financial support from working women.

If assessed on social status, the company's shareholders were as assorted as the flints it set out to manufacture; likewise the board. Apart from the three flint masters, its members included a Norfolk farmer, a shopkeeper, an innkeeper, the Brandon postmaster and a plumber.

A certificate recording the issue of four shares in the Brandon Gunflint Company in March, 1838.

Suffolk Record Office

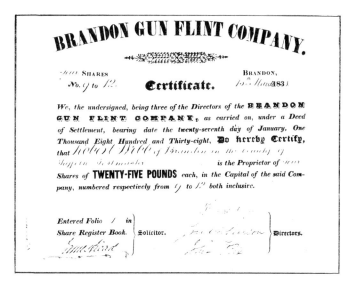

For the first three years, trade went ahead smoothly. The company paid a ten per cent. dividend on the capital invested. Shareholders smiled. But the momentum was not sustained. Exercising hindsight, one may regret that John Angerstein, assuredly well versed in business dealings, did not actively concern himself with the company's affairs, or, if aloof from heading a group of artificers, persuade a lawyer or experienced man of business to join its management. It is questionable whether the directors had the initiative or authority to reorganise the industry, force up the price of gunflints and secure not only an income for shareholders but a better livelihood for all engaged in the craft.

Instead prices asked for its products remained abysmal even after six years of trading. On 7th May, 1845, the company supplied an agent with samples of spotted musket flints priced at 2s. 3d. (11p.) per mille and samples of spotted gun flints at 1s. 3d (6p.) p.m. "We have," its representative wrote, "a stock of the former, say, Spotted Muskets about 600,000 — of the Spotted Gun about 500,000. We could do from two to three million Second Muskets at 3s. 6d. p.m."

In July that year, a letter sent to the London firm of Oxley and Taylor records an interesting transition both in gunflint transport and local railway history. No time, the writer stated, would be lost in completing the firm's order for 200,000 Common flints, but on inquiring at Brandon Station* about carriage rates, he was informed that while the line was open for passengers it would be a few days before it could accept luggage. However, he promised to advise the firm immediately this facility was available and, meanwhile, acknowledged an order it had given the company's representative in London for:

1,000,000 bulk Common Musket at 2s. p.m.
1,000,000 Second Musket at 3s. p.m.
  500,000 Second Carbine at 3s. 4d. p.m.
  500,000 Common Carbine at 2s. 4d. p.m.

However distressed by over-production or low returns, the Gunflint Company never doubted that its flints were superior in quality to any manufactured elsewhere in the world. A belief, too, in their commercial excellence accompanies a letter of 29th November, 1845, to Phillips and Diplady, brokers at George Yard in Lombard Street, London, then buying flints for the Wolverhampton merchants, Thomas Ewell and Sons. "We had these Muskets made on purpose for you," the letter ran, "and we doubt not you will upon examining them pronounce them to be the best you ever purchased for the money."

Demands for samples could be irksome, and even bedevil profits, since the company bore their cost and carriage. Patience was needed when dealing with customers who challenged or misunderstood its descriptions. On 13th January, 1847, Frederick Barnes & Company, Birmingham merchants, received by rail samples of Horse Pistols, Muskets and Fowling flints, for which prices asked were Second Musket 4s. (20p.) p.m., Best Horse Pistol 3s. 5d. (17p.) p.m. and Fine Fowling 3s. 6d. (17½p.) p.m. "These are the qualities," the company said, "we are supplying to the East India trade." There was some ambiguity, the merchants felt, about the company's description of another of its lines, bulk common flints. What were they? These gunflints, it was explained, were never manufactured "all sizeable". Had they been so at the price quoted "the workmen could not earn bread for their families." Nevertheless, the merchants were assured, such flints would be 20 per cent. better in quality than Burgon (the company's London-based rival, a potential monopolist, with a flintworks in Brandon) could supply. Common Muskets were

---

*The station was new. *A Guide to the Norfolk Railway,* 1845, describes it as standing on the right of the line, a handsome building of black flint edged with grey stone and bricks similar to that at Thetford and built precisely on the plan of the Attleborough Station.

then available at 2s. 9d. (14p.) all bulk, one half of which, the company claimed, equalled Burgon's Seconds; common bulk Horse Pistol at 1s. 9d. (9p.) p.m., Seconds at 2s. 3d. (11½p.) p.m., common bulk Fowling at 1s. 8d. (8½p.) p.m., and Seconds at 2s. 3d. (11½p.). p.m.

One muddle-headed request came from a firm asking for flints small size, say 20 mille, in a small cask. All straightforward. But the flint sent as a specimen was a Horse Pistol, and 20 thousand Horse Pistols, as the company pointed out, weighed 3 cwt. and cost 2s. 9d. (14p.) p.m. — hardly a quantity that even a magician could pack into a small cask. So it asked the would-be buyer if he required twenty thousand of these flints or twenty thousand Common Gun at 1s. 9d. (9p.) p.m., and in future dealings, felt confusion might be avoided if price and description of the sort of flints required were stated.

Inevitably, the company fell behind once its stocks got far ahead of sales. Its holdings on 26th March, 1847, amounted to:

1,000,000 Spotted Musket
460,000 Super Musket
400,000 Second Musket
150,000 Blk Common Musket
1,000,000 Blk Second Musket
200,000 Second Carbine
200,000 Super Horse Pistol
200,000 Second Horse Pistol
200,000 Super Carbine (gauged)
800,000 Fine Double Gun
350,000 Second Single
250,000 Second Double
600,000 Spotted Gun at 1s. p.m.
_____
5,810,000

If 2s. 6d. (12½p.) p.m. be reckoned their average value, that stock of gunflints lying idle locked up a capital sum in excess of £700 which was badly needed to meet wages and expenses. A forlorn outlook crept into the company's office, substantiated by unpaid bills for haulage, rail carriage, hoops for casks, casks, barrels and kegs, advertisements, agent's commission and blacksmith's services for making or repairing tools. Discord as well as embarrassment preceded the final break-up.

While some masters withdrew, others soldiered on with self-interest uppermost in their dealings. Just occasionally protest struck a positive note, even a bid to raise prices in a strictly regulated market. Conditioned by inflationary leaps, we find it hard today to appreciate the nearly static values attached to merchandise 150 years ago. For example, on 29th July, 1848, Thomas Ewell & Sons, the Wolverhampton merchants, were told: "I shall complete your remaining orders at 3s. 9d. p.m., but beg to state I shall not be able to do Sealing Flints No. 18 less than 4s. p.m. for cash in future."

John Snare kept going to the last. But when he penned that gentle ultimatum, recorded in the company's final letter book, it was too late to push up prices and stave off bankruptcy. The company, launched so optimistically, folded up in 1849, and again the manufacture and sale of Brandon's gunflints passed to individual masters.

As sometimes happens after a business has closed, a big order arrived out of the blue. The British Army by then regarded flintlocks as being as old fashioned as halberds or longbows, but countries lacking an up-to-date arms industry continued to equip their forces with muskets, carbines and flintlock pistols. Shortly before the Crimean War the Turkish Government ordered from Brandon 11,000,000 carbine flints. The suddenness of this demand, apart from its scale, implied urgency. It was also surprising, since Turkey, like Egypt, possessed her own gunflint makers. They relied, however, on surface chipping, a process at once ancient and tedious, producing flints of poor quality. Higher skills possibly existed. For farms in some Turkish villages still

R. J. Snare's flintworks in Thetford Road, Brandon, on 18th August, 1878. Each process, quartering, flaking and knapping, is shown in this self-conscious picture.

Photograph lent by Mr Albert Wing

adopted a practice reminiscent of the Roman *tribulum*, "a sharp threshing instrument having teeth". To flat slabs of wood about six feet in length, they fixed rows of well-cut flint blades. Dragged by oxen, the "threshing sledge", on which the driver stood, bumped to and fro across the harvest floor, winnowing grain and shredding straw.

The Snare family picked up the Turkish order smartly. Once again hammers struck musical notes in knapping shops and stone diggers resumed their burrowings inside the black and white world of Lingheath.

While global demands for gunflints fluctuated or defied prediction, cottages and houses continued to be built with flint walls, the flints random or faced, in the latter case rounded or squared. The building industry absorbed thousands of tons, and flint chips, the debris from knapping yards, provided sound foundations for buildings or railway tracks. So local outlets did not dry up. Nor, despite the phosphorous match, was it yet time to write off the tinderbox with its touchwood, flint and steel.

Because of the illiteracy that dogged some flint-masters and knappers, the industry evolved its own code for recording gunflints and invoicing for flints sold. Just one numeral was used, the figure 7, because, so folklore asserts, its shape resembled a miner's pick. For the rest, the code relied on strokes or dashes, uprights, diagonals and crosses, and what passes mathematically for the minus sign. To signify 1000, X was used, and any 1 following it indicated 100; thus XIII was 1300, and XIHI 1500, the diagonal altering the four to five. A minus sign indicated the addition of half the previous figure. So a cask marked XXI— contained 2,150 gunflints and one chalked XXX7I— held 3,850.

The flint master used a different set of symbols to make out his bills. A circle (0) stood for £1 sterling, but a circle with a line through its centre (Θ) was 10s. (50p.); an upright stroke was now a penny, and a minus sign a halfpenny. The same figure 7 was admitted, and a diagonal across four uprights or strokes was five. So anyone presented with a bill for 000. Θ IHI — was expected to pay £3 10s. 5½d.

Jags of flint were also recorded by cabalistic signs, but these varied slightly from shop to shop; some works marked a jag thus ᴐ , others adopted a mere curve ᴖ , but none denoted half a jag by a minus sign, almost all using a side curve (for such a measure.

The speed at which craftsmen split and trimmed flint seemed painfully slow in contrast to a teller totalling the day's output or filling barrels. He counted always in casts of five, picking up two gunflints in his left hand and three in his right, the action one of whizzing dexterity as if he were giving a demonstration of sleight of hand. A practised teller worked at the rate of 500 gunflints a minute; a maestro could reach 600.

The fives habit persists. But in modern times, once a knapper cast 200

ROBERT JOHN SNARE
(Late R. CURSON & MOUNT),
MANUFACTURER of MILITARY & SPORTING BLACK GUN-FLINTS,
WHOLESALE AND FOR EXPORTATION.

Merchants and the Trade supplied with every description of Gun-Flints of good quality, on Terms as reasonable as any House in the Trade. Also, Ornamental Flint for Building Purposes.

N.B.—R. J. S. is the most extensive Manufacturer of these Goods in England.

A large quantity of good Road Material for Concrete or other purposes always on hand.

BRANDON, SUFFOLK.

An advertisement for R. J. Snare's flint business which appeared in White's *Directory of Suffolk,* 1885.   *Suffolk Record Office*

flints to fill a bag, he placed it on his scales and used it as a counterweight, like a bank cashier, while bagging up equal parcels to total, say, 5,000 gunflints of the same sort. The former shorthand adopted for marking up barrels, submitting bills or recording jags has died out.

By 1868, three masters controlled the Brandon industry, which then engaged about thirty-six men in its knapping shops and depended for its supplies of raw flint on a handful of men and boys mining on Lingheath. Territories serviced ranged from China to the Andes, and such was the variety of flintlocks exported or in current use on a world front that these shops turned out gunflints in twenty-three different patterns.

These gunflint varieties, as James Wyatt noted them, consisted of: 1 Small Common Gun, 2 Second Single, 3 Fine Single, 4 Super Single, 5 Super Double, 6 Fine Pocket Pistol, 7 Super Pocket Pistol, 8 Second Double, 9 Fine Double, 10 Second Horse Pistol, 11 Best Horse Pistol, 12 Double-Edge Horse Pistol, 13 Double-Edge Carbine, 14 Double-Edge Musket, 15 Second Carbine, 16 Best Carbine, 17 Black Common Musket, 18 Second Musket, 19 Best Musket, 20 Grey Musket, 21 Large Common Gun, 22 Common Carbine and 23 Grey Mixed Musket. Knappers also trimmed large flakes into two shapes specifically for strike-a-lights.

William Curson, who brought out a catalogue in 1865, defined his trade as manufacturing flints "for the American, South American, Indian, West Indian, African and Cape of Good Hope markets". His cheapest line consisted of his common African gunflints for sale at 1s. 9d (9p.) to 2s. (10p.) per mille,

84

and the most highly priced his Extra Superfine Black Rifle flints, for which he was asking 5s. (25p.) p.m. Altogether, he advertised his running stock as two million fabricated in nineteen sorts from Pocket Pistols to Extra Large Muskets or Sealing Gunflints.

Long after most fur hunters had modernised their armouries, white sealers in Greenland were loth to discard flintlocks. Some experimented with the percussion caps when first introduced, but found it impossible in freezing conditions to fit a cap to the cartridge primer. The cap had to lie flush with a steel nipple, and attempts to fit the cap while wearing thick gloves required an almost superhuman dexterity. Until the self-contained cartridge obviated this difficulty huge numbers of seals continued to be killed by men darting over the icefields with flintlocks fired by Brandon gunflints.

By 1878 the industry mustered no more than twenty-six men and boys occupied in four knapping shops and relying as formerly on supplies from a few "independents" rootling flint out of Lingheath's chalk. A decline in knappers did not augur a slump in demand. On the contrary, merchants in London, Birmingham, Sheffield, Liverpool, Bristol and Hull could have marketed larger supplies than the country's one manufacturing centre then produced. Yet, despite a drop in production, flint prices never rocketed.

Black gunflints knapped from Lingheath's "floorstone" remained the prime requirement. Strangely, where tribes adopted flints as barter tokens, merchants had a poor response when attempting to sell spotted or grey-coloured flints. The natives believed their stony currency was valid only if black. In some Brandon shops, until well into this century, tins were set aside for "greys and chalks". It was then a boy's job to duff them, dipping his brush into a pot of lampblack and blacking out their spots.

A flint shop, showing the tins in which different sizes of gunflint were put. In the foreground can be seen a small tin containing lampblack and a brush for duffing spotted flints to suit the African market. *Herbert Field collection*

The decline in knapping strength in the seventies, revealing perhaps a preference by the town's youngsters for outdoor work, cannot, I think, be directly attributed to the industry's toll of lungs and life. French flint workers were alive to the health hazards of knapping, but this realisation came slowly to Brandon. Commenting on the legend that most knappers died of consumption round about forty, Sydney Skertchly felt that their early deaths had more to do with drink than with flint, especially as knappers customarily worked from Wednesday to Saturday, the prelude, perhaps, to a long boozy weekend.

That drink overthrew flint-working breadwinners in a number of families cannot be doubted. Elderly men in Brandon today recall a rush of knappers to the *One Bell*, a pub in the High Street, whenever they had a sovereign or two, not necessarily to spare, in their "long melfords", stocking-like leather purses. When they staggered out, sosh-wise or not, few had resources left except a feeling of being well tanked up. During the bread riots of 1816, male members of the mob shouted for beer, but their womenfolk cried out in protest, fearful of the consequences.

As the age's main source of village entertainment, the pub offered the worker a warm friendly atmosphere, a haven alike from dull and irksome toil. The bar with its gossip, jokes and games enriched conviviality, apart from its refreshments. But flint knappers had a more cogent reason for their

V. R. "Vic" Edwards demonstrating the point of contact while trimming a flint against the iron stake or anvil fixed to his block.
Herbert Field collection

86

patronage. Flint and chalk dust inhaled all day set up a burning thirst that just had to be satisfied.

There were always exceptions. Some of the steadiest men in Brandon, Skertchly found, were elderly knappers. He noted a practice in some shops of damping down flint to reduce the chalk dust, but admitted, perhaps against his convictions, that "particles of flint dust flying about had an effect on health."

In 1874, three Snares managed gunflint manufacturing businesses in Brandon, all of them operating from buildings in Thetford Road. Robert John Snare, with the largest flintworks in town, specialised in ornamental flints as well as gunflints, but only gunflints concerned John Snare and Mrs. Lucy Eunice Snare.

In the same road, James Field then headed another Brandon family whose descendants, if not their forbears, suffered heavily for adhering to this dusty craft. As well as manufacturing gunflints, he ran a whiting works, a painting of which, showing a horse turning his chalk mill, is cherished by his great grandson. And, as additional grist for his shop and mill, he managed the *Fox & Hounds*, a pub since rebuilt and renamed *The Forest*.

Robert Snare shipped flints in large quantities to Africa, packed as a rule in old flour barrels, 29,000 to a barrel. His main supplies were landed at Zanzibar, from where dealers or fortune hunters hired porters to carry them into the interior. In a six-year period the output of the R. J. Snare manufactory exceeded twenty million gunflints, the actual return which he gave to Edward Lovett being:

1880	4,500,000
1881	2,832,500
1882	3,115,000
1883	4,721,300
1884	4,793,150
1885	3,203,250
	23,165,200

On the basis of Sydney Skertchly's researches in 1876, a jag of average flint yielded 6,000 gunflints, a jag of good flint 12,000 and one of exceptional flint up to 18,000, but that figure would include many of pocket pistol size. Therefore, 23 million flints knapped in this one Snare Shop probably absorbed at least 2,000 tons of raw flint, every nodule or slab of it mined, stone by stone, from Lingheath's pits.

On the threshold of the eighties, scientists suddenly took an interest in the industry's alleged antiquity. J. Park Harrison, reporting to the British Association for the Advancement of Science, supposed that flint knappers and their families in Brandon as well as other members of the town's population were a race apart. Their dark hair, dark eyes and depressed nasal bones contrasted with the rest of the people of Norfolk and Suffolk. In support of his point, he instanced physical characteristics lately recorded of recruits to the West Norfolk Regiment. Of eighty men whose personal sheets he studied, three only had dark hair and eyes, and seventeen a depressed nasal bone. These Brandon inhabitants, he felt, could easily be taken for Welsh, and some French anthropologists, when shown their photographs, thought they resembled Iberian types. To this scientist, if to no other, the short swarthy figures he reported on represented survivals of an early pre-Celtic race.

Fitting a flint into a gunlock.
James English collection

Trade went on booming into the nineties. True, contracts originating from the South American market fell away, especially those from Brazil, but increased exports to South Africa, then a fast developing country, filled most gaps caused by Brazilian withdrawals. Visiting Brandon in 1892, the essayist P. Anderson Graham got the impression of "a most flourishing and active industry", despite the latest invention of hammerless breechloaders. The knappers and miners to whom he spoke convinced him of their craft's deep-seated traditions, each exercising skills inherited from his forebears.

Out on the heath, he recorded: "There is a patriarch over seventy still to be seen on sunny days hanging about the chalk pits, though totally unfit to wield the spade or pick. Before the fir trees were planted that now overshadow some of the white mounds, he remembers coming to help his father and grandsire, while close at hand his son and grandson are at work."

That simple scene admirably summarises the Ashley family's devotion to stone digging through five generations.

CHAPTER EIGHT

Evaluators of Brandon's Gunflint Industry

A T different periods geologists, archaeologists and other specialists set out to discover and record the technical skills, the hazards and the trading outlets as well as historic or prehistoric foundations underlying Brandon's gunflint industry. Their observations, occasionally quixotic, constitute lively pictures of men pursuing a traditional craft in a small, close-knit community.

Mr Seymour de Lotbiniere lives at Brandon Hall, a William and Mary building of red brick and grey flint, the bright look of which is not, like all-flint walls, rendered sombre by rain. With the advantage of local contacts and a fifty-year familiarity with knappers and their ways, he has, I think, devoted more time and thought than anyone to the industry's origin and growth at both national and local levels.

The earliest chronicler on the scene, Dr James Mitchell, a Scottish geologist, visited Brandon a year or two before its Gunflint Company was formed and recorded his findings in the *New Edinburgh Review* in 1837. The industry was then in a distressed state after its bonanza towards the end of the Napoleonic Wars. Gunflints earned, he was told, 7s. 6d. (37½p.) a thousand as opposed to two guineas (£2.10) during palmy days. Their prices had already fallen appreciably lower and were to slump again.

The stone diggers who hauled up flints by hand from the chalky bowels of Lingheath used no machinery. They were, he felt, too poor to equip themselves with a windlass or haulage system. As he noted, their pits descended to depths of about thirty feet, and broke into three strata of flint, sometimes four. At each level of flint they pursued it horizontally, i.e. on "gain", for about twenty yards. Later practice confined tunnelling to "floor-stone" level only, with burrows seldom forking more than twelve yards from a shaft's toe. The diggers "grievously complained" about the heavy toll demanded by the parish, 5s. (25p.) for every cartload of flint extracted. A cartload consisted of "as much as three horses can draw", in effect a substantial load.

Looking on the brighter side, diggers might be thought fortunate to strike flint of excellent quality at a reasonable depth. In France, as Dr Mitchell knew from Citizen Dolomieu's researches, twenty beds of flint might lie piled one on top of another, of which two or three only yielded flint fit for knapping.

Gunflint makers at Maidstone had a similar tale to tell. For only one good stratum of flint existed, he was told, in the greenish chalk of Kentish quarries.

With the assiduity of the educated Scot, Dr Mitchell examined each phase of flint craftwork, beginning with the quarterer or "cracker", as he called him. A flaker whom he watched dropped his flakes into three casks, one for each type of flake, large size, medium and small, from which a knapper trimmed different sorts of gunflints, Carbine, Horse Pistol, Single Barrel, Double Barrel and Pistol. "The napper (sic) uses a hammer which is merely a plate of steel, extending two inches on each side of the handle, and an inch in breadth and not above a sixth of an inch in thickness. He takes into his left hand one of

A core with the flakes reattached, after Skertchly. The bulbs of percussion at the point where the core was struck are clearly visible.

the flakes, and lays it over the little anvil on the block and with his hammer breaks it into three or four flints. All he has to do after that is to see which edge will be best for the flint, and from the other he breaks a little off and the whole is complete."

Brandon's masters left him in no doubt that their gunflints had no peer, a judgment with which he agreed. They lasted longer than other gunflints, and were "most certain in their fire."

What, however, especially distinguishes Dr Mitchell's contribution is his testimony to the mode of flaking practised by the town's craftsmen. It was the French mode, and this, he affirmed, had been their custom for about forty years. Skilful use of a pointed French hammer, when applied to good running flint, resulted in flakes six to eight inches in length, either double or single backed, with equal flanges. This transition into what Mr de Lotbiniere calls the "platform technique" ousted the former wedge system in which knappers, using a round-headed English hammer, struck off flakes of all sizes and shapes and trimmed them almost willy-nilly. The advantages of the platform technique are plain; a more economical use of flint, easier working, less trimming for knappers, accelerated production.

The next observer on the scene, James Wyatt, also a geologist, came from Bedford. A practical man, able to knap in the Neolithic manner with a pointed stone, he put on a knapper's apron in a Brandon flint shop and, as his editor, Edward Stevens, who published his report in *Flint Chips* in 1870, wrote, "with moderate application he might succeed in earning ten or twelve shillings a week at the trade."

In the late 1860's, Wyatt's attention was called to a small flint industry at Catton, north of Norwich, then being worked by the Brandon emigré, Frewer.

A knapping hammer trimming a flake held against the knapper's stake or anvil, with the staging below to cushion any follow-through.
James English collection

But, as he expressed it, "the chief manufactory is at Brandon where it has been carried on for centuries." The precise nature of this centuries-old activity is not stated, though it was, he thought, "the best evidence of commercial activity that can be produced anywhere", the continuity of which was directly related to "implements of the drift fashioned by the old flint folk."

Although the industry was then turning out twenty-three sorts of gunflints, as well as strike-a-lights and face cubes for ornamental work, its future struck him as extremely uncertain. He doubted if it could survive beyond the next generation. At this time, flint masters were paying 6s. 6d. (32½p.) a jag to stone diggers, added to which the groundage or royalty due to Lingheath's Trustees was 1s. 8d. (8p.) and carters charged 1s. 10d. (9p.) a jag to transport stone from the heath. So each jag of raw flint, unloaded in his backyard, cost a master 10s. (50p.).

It was the prices paid for gunflints that kept men working in the industry close to the breadline, if not below it. True, there was a massive spin-off of material, the wasted flint chips, sold as top dressing for tracks, and heavier

A close-up of squared building flints used in the Guildhall at Norwich, one of the finest examples of medieval flint construction. *Terry Moore*

stone reappeared in house walls. Flints squared as facing stones, chiefly for churches, averaged 2s. 9d (13½p.) a cwt. Wyatt was more surprised, though, by the low average price paid for gunflints, about 4s (20p.) a thousand. He wondered how men lived by a craft that entailed so much labour for so little money.

In some shops, aged men and boys were employed making strike-a-lights out of large flakes which the flakers had rejected as unsuitable for trimming into gunflints. They cut these into circular discs about two inches in diameter, such employment for boys foreshadowing perhaps a working lifetime ahead at a knapping block.

As scrupulously as Dr Mitchell had done, Wyatt detailed each manufacturing process. The quarterer used, he saw, a small round-faced hammer, called the English hammer, to dress up a block (quarter), removing the rind or rough white skin from one side to get a surface from which flakes could be struck. To flake "the workman rests the mass of flint on his left knee and with one smart tap on the corner of the flint — the hammer being directed at an angle of about 45 degrees — strikes off a flake the whole depth of the flint if its running quality be good."

A good flaker, he said, could turn out about 9,000 flakes in a day's work, about 7,000 being the average output. This quantity kept three knappers busy. He noticed how adept some men had become. Bent over their knapping blocks, sometimes with no more than a solitary candle on a winter's night, they produced just as many gunflints as in midsummer.

Wyatt found a peculiar joy in listening to the tinkle, tinkle of falling flints as the knapping hammers rose and fell in rhythmical movements, chip striking chip, and trimmed flints pitching on others when tossed into tubs. Each percussive stroke had a musical ring, counterpointed by a light thump as the knapper's hammer followed through and rebounded from the leatherwork beside the iron stake.

He considered the standard of gunflint production in Brandon higher than in France. The French were knapping but one gunflint from each flake, whereas Brandon craftsmen hammered out two or three, sometimes four, from a single flake. Such workings attest their expertise as flakers and knappers, but it is equally a testimony to the homogeneous, smooth-running texture of their mineral, the ages-respected, ages-renowned, silky black "floorstone".

Despite his appraisal of their craft skills, Wyatt insisted that no Brandonian, however dexterous, had ever produced or could produce "the beautiful, conchoidal waves, crimpings and ripple work displayed on the surface of tools and weapons found in Scandinavia, and on the barbs and arrow points of a still earlier period." Had he seen the Hindsgavl dagger recovered from Northern Funen, Denmark, his admiration for rippled

The Hindsgavl dagger, a masterpiece of Neolithic flint craft.
National Museum, Copenhagen

flintwork might have taken wing. A masterpiece of the late Neolithic Age, indeed one of the world's finest examples of flint craft, it is modelled on bronze daggers imported probably from the Mediterranean. The National Museum, Copenhagen, bought it in 1923 from the estate of the late owner of Hindsgavl Manor, Fyn. Nothing is known of the year or circumstances of the find. But, as the museum says, in workmanship this dagger is flawless and superb; it is made with the greatest care as to proportions (length 29.5 cm) and decorative effect.

The next evaluator was Sydney Barber Josiah Skertchly who died, after a long and distinguished life, at Molendinar, Queensland, on 2nd February, 1926.* Passionately fond of delving in pits, gravel-rash being his earliest remembered ailment, he spent part of his boyhood at Ashby-de-la-Zouch, immortalised by *Ivanhoe*. He received tuition from the scientist T. H. Huxley, and Charles Darwin praised his work. After leaving England, and before settling in Australia in 1894, he visited tribes in remote settlements such as the Red Cloud Indians at Mount Shasta, California, studying their craftsmanship and collecting specimens, lived among Dyaks in Borneo, travelled in China, and was for a period Professor of Botany at Hongkong. A man of the liveliest character, full of quirks and indiscretions, he subjected Brandon's industry to the most searching scrutiny in the years 1875-78, while working for the Geological Survey.

Skertchly rented a cottage, the Lode, the north wall of which I described in chapter one. Its appearance delighted him. He thought it had been built twenty years before he moved in and said that if it was demolished, its black flints would give knappers good value. To lend weight to his purpose, he took a share in a flint mine and entered into partnership with J. W. Southwell, then about the cleverest knapper in the town but, as he soon discovered, "an untamed savage of delightful personality". Southwell was also a poacher of uncommon mettle until sadly someone knocked him on the head and his body was dragged out of the Little Ouse.

Skertchly's work, a small masterpiece of industrial research, was published in 1879 as a memoir of the Geological Survey of England and Wales at the then stiff price of 17s. 6d. (87½p.). It had the resounding title of:

On the Manufacture of Gun-Flints
The Methods of Excavation for Flint
The Age of Palaeolithic Man
and
The Connexion between Neolithic Art
and the Gun-Flint Trade.

*During the last thirty years of his life, when settled in South-east Queensland, Skertchly took an interest in the Queensland Museum in Fortitude Valley, and presented it with a valuable collection of specimens which he catalogued in plain, immensely readable language. They include artefacts and flint items from Grime's Graves, Snake Wood, the Little Ouse River, Brandon Beds, West Stow, Eriswell, Icklingham, Mildenhall, Broomhill and Warren Hill, all sites in the Brandon district.

A group of Neolithic arrow heads and a fish hook all cut from flint.

National Museum, Copenhagen

In its eighty pages, he ranges over the craft's ancient origins, a topic he liked to develop with almost obsessive zeal, the geographical distribution of black flint, tools used by Lingheath and Neolithic miners, their methods of sinking shafts and tunnelling, differences between English and French mining and knapping practices, the fire power of gunflints (how many discharges a good flint should spark off steel), different sorts of gunflints, strike-a-lights, and affinities between a 4,000-year-old craft and mid-Victorian flint craft. Only a perfectionist, exercising hindsight, could ask for more; perhaps mortality tables, some survey of family histories or records, and a discussion of flaking angles.

With the advantage of a year as librarian and diagram-maker at the Geological Society, Skertchly readily applied himself to defining and drawing the different sorts of gunflints. Of 71 illustrations in his work, 35 represent manufactured flints, starting with Wall Piece, Large Swan and Best Musket and concluding with Old English Gun-Flint, French Gun-Flint, Cut and

Polished Gun-Flint and German Gun-Flint. He accompanied each diagram with measurements and a detailed description of the flint's characteristics.

Having defined a jag as a "one-horse cart load about equal to a ton", Skertchly set out to discover exactly how many gunflints a jag of average quality would yield. Whether he followed a load direct from his mine at Lingheath to his partner's flintworks is not known. But there, in their shop, we may visualise him sitting notebook in hand, counting and tracing each nodule's fractures, wasteful and useful, to the very last knap. This brilliant inquiry elicited the following table:

	Number	Weight		
		Cwt.	St.	Lbs.
Flakes	8,800			
Gun-Flints		1	6	0
including				
Second Muskets	550			
Common Black Muskets	500			
Common Grey do	150			
Second Carbines	4,100			
Common do	1,900			
Horse Pistols	2,000			
Singles	400			
Large Guns	750			
Small do	500			
Faced Builders	60	0	6	13
Rough do	210	3	3	4
Chips	—	6	7	12
		13	0	1

His mentor, the adroit knapper and artful poacher, proved able to identify his own gunflints by touch. For Southwell had no difficulty when blindfolded in picking out flints which he had knapped from an assortment containing work by others. But, as if to demonstrate a refinement of this touch, he identified some gunflints as his partial manufacture, recognising that he had finished them off whereas Skertchly, or someone else, had started to trim them. To unpractised eyes, all gunflints of a particular sort look much alike.

The same painstaking attention was given to flint pits. Wherever this indefatigable geologist/botanist located them, active or disused, he measured the different geological strata penetrated and depths at which the coveted "floorstone" was reached. At Santon Downham, near Blood Hill, close to the Little Ouse, this flint seam was a mere ten feet below the surface.

Close to the River Lark at Icklingham, a village ten miles south of Brandon, there had been, he thought, some Neolithic activity, but more conspicuously, extensive shaft workings in the 1830s. The flint dug out of chalk there caused knappers for a period to desert their Brandon shops, set up sheds or shelters beside the pits and work on site, travelling back to their cottages at weekends. The flint so available was jackdaw coloured, free of impurities and of good running quality, in short, lovely stuff. When he and Southwell visited Icklingham, they found its site scarred by perhaps 500 pits, but abandoned except by one knapper in the neighbourhood, Henry Ashley, of the Brandon stone-digging family. In 1876 he had not worked flint for two years, but up to 1874 he had both mined and knapped flint at Icklingham to reduce haulage costs.

Skertchly followed up Canon Greenwell's discoveries at Grime's Graves, made only six years earlier, and reached firm conclusions about links in craftsmanship between its Neolithic knappers and those in Brandon's shops. There was a resemblance, too, he felt, between their ethnic groups. But more convincingly, the gunflint, he argued, evolved from the medieval strike-a-light, and this in turn owed its genesis to the Neolithic scraper.

What struck him also as significant were differences in practices between French *caillouteurs* and Suffolk flint workers. As he pointed out, nineteenth-century Brandon and Neolithic miners worked a number of pits close together, sank shafts direct to the "floorstone", burrowed horizontally from a pit's base within a radius of about twelve yards, filled in worked out burrows with chalk rubble and used a single-pronged pick. The French did none of this. Again, before English knappers adopted the French mode of flaking, both Brandon man and Neolithic man used a round-headed hammer—in the latter case a stone—whereas the French opted for a square-headed or pointed hammer. Neither did they manufacture oval or horseshoe strike-a-lights, nor undercut the sides of their flints.

Though basically the difference between Brandon's craftsmen and their ancient forerunners might be the substitution of iron and steel for bone, antler and stone as mining and knapping tools, one would be rash to attribute French practices to their lack of a Grime's Graves background. The controversy which Skertchly sparked off refuses to die.

Another to evaluate the industry perceptively was Edward Lovett, of West Burton House, Croydon. Visiting Brandon in 1886, he recorded his observations in the *Proceedings of the Society of Antiquarians of Scotland*, March, 1887. Commendably candid, he wrote that ". . . owing to the kindness of Mr. Snare, one of the leading manufacturers of Brandon, I was able in a very short time to examine the whole history of the gunflint from the digging of the rough material to the packing up of the finished gunflints for export."

Like Skertchly, Lovett saw that Lingheath's stone diggers protected their

97

flints against weathering, throwing branches of Scots fir over heaps of freshly detached nodules as a shield against sun or frost. While watching knappers at work, he saw how precisely they trimmed their flints to particular sizes without ever using a gauge. They referred to their long flakes, he noticed, as "Frenchmen", thereby acknowledging an indebtedness of at least eighty years. In contrast, they called flints manufactured as strike-a-lights "Englishmen", as these were made on the pattern of old gunflints, rounded at the base. A tinder box trade then extended to China.

Almost an investigatory famine followed. True, several men descended on the town, wrote interesting articles about its craft, and sometimes made extravagant claims. But it was not until 1934, when the young Norfolk archaeologist, Roy Rainbird Clarke, a gifted son of Breckland's first historian, brought his discipline to Brandon that another valuable memoir on the industry resulted. Clarke published his observations in *Antiquity*, March, 1935. Although he recapitulated some of the historical documentation, his main interest lay in describing in technical detail the flint mines and the processes of gunflint manufacture, with notes about the numbers of knappers engaged, their vocabularies, the prices paid for flints, the industry's export markets and its by-products.

Inside a Brandon flint shop in 1876, with flaker and boy knapper at work and a large slab of tabular flint near the window. An engraving from a photograph, after Skertchly.

In June he measured a shaft sunk by "Pony" Ashley on Lingheath, and recorded its composition and structure through different geological levels — sands and gravel at the top, next decomposed chalk and finally hard chalk at the base. The shaft, 43 feet 6 inches deep, averaged no more than three feet by two feet, a one-man working space. To protect himself against bad weather and falling stones or sand, Ashley undercut the sides by about three feet in every fifteen feet of depth. At the toe, Clarke crawled along a main burrow to see how he exploited the "floorstone". The burrow ran "gain" for about 36 feet and ended in an apse about 12 feet in diameter and 2 feet 6 inches high, which Ashley called a "draw". If a good yield resulted, he planned to sink his next shaft straight through the roof of that "draw", and so spare himself the labour of hauling out a ton or so of disturbed, unwanted chalk.

A miner spent about a month, Clarke believed, in sinking a shaft about forty feet deep, and from six to nine months to excavate the flint from burrows tunnelled from its toe. If the initial sinking absorbed so much time, the digger faced a grim succession of penniless days, for flint masters paid only for stone raised, so much a jag. Here Clarke was, I think, misinformed. As he had seen at Grime's Graves, once the Neolithic miners reached the "floorstone", they did not dig beneath it with their antler picks, but levered it out at base level. At Lingheath, Ashley, and those who preceded him, organised their tunnels so that the flint seam faced them about head high, as they lay on their sides. They thought this the best way of detaching it.

Once again the question, so provocative of bold suppositions, had to be faced. How intimately are the historic and prehistoric industries of the district related? In drawing comparisons between modern and ancient flint workings Skertchly was, Clarke suggested, guilty of selecting his evidence. But granted fundamental differences between Grime's Graves and Lingheath in methods of shaft construction and flint extraction in their galleries, the balance of probability came down, he thought, on the geologist's side. However, his archaeological training prompted caution. Many gaps needed to be bridged, he declared, and stages in evolution explained before a continuous industrial development was admissible.

The notion of an unbroken tradition cuts no ice with Mr Seymour de Lotbiniere. He rejects it as mythical. Living in Brandon, the owner of a private gunflint museum, he has tried to sift historical truth from fiction in his researches. His father, Brigadier-General Joly de Lotbiniere, purchased Brandon Hall shortly after service with the Canadian Army in the First World War. The town's "ancient industry" attracted him in boyhood. Enthralled, he watched that doyen of knapping masters, Fred Snare, handling flints. The old knapper gave him copies or imitations of prehistoric weapons and sometimes accompanied him to the Little Ouse where the two searched its banks for microliths (tiny flakes used perhaps for scraping arrow shafts smooth) and other Neolithic relics. With his brother, Mr de Lotbiniere took torches, candles and ropes to Grime's Graves and explored its partially accessible but excavated pits long before one was equipped with a metal ladder and opened for public inspection. Dropping to "floorstone" level, the two boys groped on hands and knees through cluttered galleries abandoned some time between 2500 and 1500 BC. On their father's death in 1960, Brandon Hall passed out of the family. But Mr de Lotbiniere bought it back in 1968, and since his retirement from the BBC, having been Director of Outside Broadcasts and later a Television Controller, has missed few chances of developing his hobby interest.

"I concentrated," he said, "on the public side, especially the military as it's reasonably well documented, whereas if you look into the private side — records kept by country landowners, estate agents, farmers, game-keepers and the like — you'll find the material too scattered. As such archives are mainly family ones, it's unlikely there would be much about gunflints."

The military historian on the other hand can consult a huge library of books and records devoted to flintlock weapons in English, French, German, Danish, Dutch and other languages. But very few, it seems, however en-cyclopaedic, make more than a passing reference to the flints used, their source of origin and manufacture.

Absence of such information stimulated Mr de Lotbiniere's researches. Apart from long sessions at the Public Record Office, Kew, sifting through Board of Ordnance documents, he examined records of the East India Company in London, those of the Hudson's Bay Company in Winnipeg, took his inquiries to the Tower of London's Armouries, to museums in Maidstone, Salisbury and Dorchester, former centres of gunflint manufacture, and to sites in Denmark, Holland, Belgium and France where flints had been mined and worked. At home, whenever he saw old flint buildings, among them knappers' cottages, being demolished to make way for a bungalow civilisation, he asked foremen and clerks of works to look out for and save any trimmed flints spotted during excavations.

For coming generations, he has built up an archive of photographs, maps and diagrams covering more than a century of localised flintcraft, knapping procedures, technical equipment, the layout of the town's main flintworks, and mining at Lingheath. The most fascinating aspect of his hobby, however, rests with his collection of gunflints and manufacturing tools, English and French, for these demonstrate the gunflint's evolution since the Duke of Marlborough's campaigns. The flints fall into two distinctive categories, those of "wedge" manufacture, the early form of English gunflint, and those with double backs for which he invented the term "platform manufacture", because of their elevated but flat table-like tops, the results of being knapped from long flakes struck by a pointed French-type hammer.

A glimpse into a flint shop of 1876, with two knappers surrounded by flint chips, and in the foreground a group of quartering and flaking hammers. An engraving from a photograph, after Skertchly.

Historic flints lie in his showcases. There are "double backs" from Acre, Palestine, which are probably British gunflints. Napoleon attacked the town in 1799, as incidental to his Egyptian campaign, but the Turks garrisoning its castle resisted his siege, and afterwards it emerged that they had drawn on gunflints obtained from a British ship. He has gunflints salvaged from famous wrecks, including Sir Clowdesley Shovell's flagship, the *Association*, lost off the Scilly Isles in 1707; H.M.S. *Colossus*, which foundered in a storm off the same dangerous coast in December, 1798, its stores including eight cases of Sir William Hamilton's precious Greek vases; the *Abergavenny*, sunk in 1805; and the schooner *Douro*, lost in 1842. The most intriguing flints in his collection, however, are some British Muskets, almost certainly of Brandon manufacture, which he picked up while walking over Huguemont Farm, the focal point of Wellington's strategy at Waterloo.

Among his varied services to Brandon, Mr de Lotbiniere has conferred prestige on the flintknapping craft, though he disclaims credit for it. "Once," he said, "people were shy, a little ashamed of admitting descent from a flintknapper; today they are rather proud of it."

According to his records, the craft dynasty founded by John Snare, who died in 1824, represents the strongest link any Brandon family has with gunflint manufacture. It runs unbroken through five generations. John Snare owned a limeburning business, and quarried a deep chalk pit for his material. This, Mr de Lotbiniere suggests, could have brought him face to face with the black flint seam, the craft's mainstay. The Carter family, also prominent flint workers in the twentieth century, spread their skills over four generations, and the Edwards and Fields likewise have ancient forebears rooted in flint. However, all his discoveries reinforce his conviction that the gunflint industry was not established as an organised craft in Brandon before 1790.

His researches, too, suggest that it was largely an influx of craftsmen from outside East Anglia, men mainly from Kent and Wiltshire (two counties much concerned with gunflint production in the eighteenth century), who moved into Brandon, eager to exploit its rare black flint. Wherever they originated, and they included men from north-west Kent as well as William Southwell from a Hampshire village, these newcomers required only a few years to transform a quiet township, living largely on rabbits — 40,000 from one warren in one year reached London's markets — into the gunflint arsenal of the British Army and Navy. Was it merely opportunism that prompted Philip Hayward, first heard of as a flint manufacturer at Bury St Edmunds, to buy Flint Hall, Brandon, and set up alongside cottages and workshops for knappers?

Another big question remains: Who first with a gunflint industry in mind grasped the advantages, ultimately proved unrivalled, of the locality's fine-textured, intrusion-free, easy-running black flint? That individual deserves a statue on Market Hill.

Until early in the nineteenth century, parents were under no legal obligation when registering a child's birth to state the occupation of its father. But in 1813, as Mr de Lotbiniere discovered, twenty-three out of sixty-two newly baptised children in Brandon had flintknappers as fathers, and several of them had names like Oxley, Peverett and Rissbrook, unknown in Brandon in earlier centuries. It could be that our statue to the industry's founder might commemorate one who, in East Anglian reckoning, would be "a furriner".

As for the belief that knappers once left Brandon to work in churchyards, trimming flints to decorate medieval churches as they were being built in Norfolk and Suffolk, Mr de Lotbiniere thinks that is unlikely. "Look at Brandon's church of St Peter," he said, "a fourteenth-century structure, and you will not find ornamental flintwork in the building. If local flint workers exercised so dominant an influence as supposed, you would not expect them to neglect their own parish church."

CHAPTER NINE

Apprentices deterred by a Killing Occupation

A S the nineteenth century faded out, demand for Brandon's gunflints continued to exceed supplies despite exports of about 4,000,000 flints a year to Africa and consignments also to China, Java, Sumatra, the Malay Archipelago and territories in Latin America. The town needed more knappers to satisfy its global markets. But many boys on leaving school looked for other jobs, deterred as much by the craft's exacting seven-year apprenticeship as by its lethal dust.

Because of falling output, prices rose higher than those obtainable two decades earlier. In 1900, gunflints manufactured in Brandon's shops were priced per thousand as follows:

	s.	d.	
Second Musket	5	6	(27½p)
Common Musket	4	6	(22½p)
Second Carbine	5	0	(25p)
Second Horse Pistol	3	6	(17½p)
Common Horse Pistol	2	9	(14p)
Second Single	3	3	(16p)
Common Carbine	4	6	(22½p)

Top quality gunflints such as Best Muskets and Best Carbines took a knock, the cheaper article dominating manufacture. According to one observer, fastidious about heights, musket flints of whatever quality measured in inches $1.3 \times 1.1 \times 0.4$; carbine size was $1.2 \times 1.0 \times 0.25$, and horse pistol $1.1 \times 1.0 \times 0.3$. Second Carbines, though double backed at this time, were single edged but slightly flawed because of bad colour, spots or an imperfect edge. Best Carbines, though also single edged, were cut from black flakes, had good square backs or platforms and a straight and fine firing edge. Common Carbines, in contrast, were knapped from inferior flint, single backed by a good ridge but liable to show a jagged firing edge.

Ironically, though wars in the flintlock age, above all the prolonged struggle between Wellington and Napoleon, put the industry on its feet, conflicts in the twentieth century, if small, boosted it, but if world-wide, paralysed it. Gunflints fell into the category of arms and no nation, not even the British, liked exporting arms to an enemy country, however liberal about supplies in peacetime. Shipments of gunflints to South Africa ceased with the Boer War. At its outset, however, the War Office ordered a sufficiency of large flints from the Snare family to equip 14,000 tinder boxes. Each tinplate box had a tight-fitting top and collapsible inner lid for snuffing out the tinder; its contents included a knapped flint, a steel bar, and inflammable material such as rag tinder or chemically impregnated cotton waste. With this equipment, troopers in the veldt lit their camp fires and, when out of range of Boer snipers, enjoyed a smoke. Each tinder box substituted, it was said, for many times its equivalent weight in matches.

At the century's turn the principal flint masters trading in Brandon were Snare, Edwards, Carter and Field. Knappers employed in their shops worked as a rule to a flat rate of 1s. 2d (6p.) a thousand gunflints (5½d. (2p.) then bought about as much as £1 in 1980). Accordingly, as these dusty men, sitting on chairs and stools in stuffy sheds, rattled out into their casks some 300 gunflints an hour, few could afford to call it a day until he had ten hours' work behind him to give him about 3s. 6d. (17½p.) for his labour.

The stone diggers of Lingheath fared worse in a monetary sense. This testimony given me by Mrs Albert Wing conveys some notion of their toils and rewards. Her father, a longstanding miner, died aged 66.

"I remember," she recorded, "my father, the late Fred Ashley, also his brother Arthur Ashley, digging pits for flints on Lingheath during the early years of my life between 1907 and 1912. They had no engineering tackle, their only tools being a spade, a pick and hammer. It took almost a week to dig a pit as this was done in stages from one platform to another. This was done to prevent the pit caving in. At the bottom of the pit they would burrow underground similar to a rabbit to find every flintstone they could. They would also pick out large lumps of chalk. These, as well as the flints, they would carry on their heads one at a time until they reached the top of the pit. Sometimes they dug a pit only to find there were no flints. Therefore they earned no money that week. They did not take a watch to work. They knew the time by how many candles they burned down the pit, one inch per hour. They sold the flint to the flint knappers for approximately 11s. (55p.) a week."

Her father and uncle liked to work close together, but not in the same pit. Then, if one ran into trouble, he could shout for help. Once an avalanche of sand and chalk fell on Arthur Ashley. His brother, roused by a rumble, followed by a faint cry, rushed to his pit, and dug him out.

"As a girl," Mrs Wing said, "I sometimes dropped into a pit and crawled along a burrow to watch father by candlelight as he picked away at the flint pieces. It was more comfortable to sit on top and dangle my legs over the hole. He nearly always heard as soon as I called out to him. His answering shout sounded strange coming from far underground. He worked a six-day week, and every morning mother made up his 'dockey' (midday meal). She packed cheese or stewed beef sandwiches into a calico holder with a draw-string top which we called his 'tommy bag' and sometimes gave him a baked rabbit. After breakfast mother always emptied the teapot into an old beer bottle for him. Cold tea was his one drink. There was no milk in it. That would have turned it sour."

Her husband and his brother, Walter Wing, crafted single-pronged picks for the miners, usually by cannibalising old iron tyres which they ripped off useless cart or tumbril wheels. The rims were heavily worn but, skilled blacksmiths both, they soon cut out a section and hammered it into a gently curved pick head, hafting it to a handle of elder wood. A new pick before the 1914-18 war cost about 5s. (25p.). Stone diggers, continually hacking away at rock-like chalk, needed sharp-ended picks. Blunt tips made their labours so much the harder.

"We used," said Mr Wing, "to sharpen their picks for them at 2d. a time, but members of the family, the Ashleys, got theirs sharpened for 1d."

All tools used in the knapping shops as well as the barrels, casks or kegs to pack flints for export were Brandon made. Knapping hammers, such as the Wing brothers manufactured, consisted of old files squared at each end and fitted with ash or hickory handles. A horseshoe nail driven through the top secured head to haft. Oak was never used as it was too rigid. Handles had to be springy. Heavier handles of identical woods were fitted to flaking hammers. These, weighing from 2 to 2½ lb, had pointed ends, symmetrically squared, and were drawn out whenever worn. Round-headed quartering hammers, much heavier and longer lasting, were also hafted with ash or hickory.

At their forge, the brothers also shaped and fitted up knapping blocks. "We liked to cut," said Mr Wing, "an oak stump about knee high and into its flat top drive the knapping stake, a piece of iron that stood about three inches above the block's level and upright, its head flat, never chisel like. Below it, we built staging, usually a leather pad mounted on bits of old broom-handle. This gave bounce to the knapper's hammer as it followed through after breaking the flake."

Trade continued in building flints for general purposes, also in faced flints for ornamental work. Long Melford Church, one of the glories of Suffolk's medieval inheritance, displays some superb flushwork on its parapets and the exterior walls of its Lady Chapel. In unison with this heritage, its new tower, when completed in 1903, contained flints brought from Brandon and Acton which were knapped in the churchyard and set in Portland cement.

Knappers had a breather when they stepped outside their shops and sat on chairs in their yards, surrounded by piles of inferior flint or discarded cores, and trimmed off the rough to knock pieces into manageable size, few larger than a man's fist, for binding into boundary, garden or cottage walls.

Builders putting up flint walls also needed a basic craft skill founded on a principle of non-selection. With a barrow load of flints beside him, a practised man scarcely glanced at the barrow but picked up the first flint to hand and fitted it into the wall. By this haphazard procedure, regularity in pattern was obviated. The finished structure then had a pleasing if wanton wildness formed by a medley of black, white, spotted and grey stones of different sizes and shapes, clean cut, roughly cut or not cut at all.

However, for the knappers in their ceaselessly tinkling shops there was no curtailing, it seemed, the hideous toll flint dust took of the their lives, aggravated in some instances by heavy drinking. With a throat feeling like a cinder track, a man could hardly be blamed for soothing it.

A close-up of a flint wall of the church of St Peter and St Paul, Eye, showing flint cores fitted into the fabric and flint chips used for galleting.

Terry Moore

Mr Herbert Field, aged 83 in 1980, started to learn the craft as a boy of eight but after leaving school spent only four and a half years as a full-time knapper before enlisting with other Brandon lads in the Norfolk Regiment. "We thought we'd settled for a bit o'fun, travelling to Norwich for drill," he said. Wounded on the Somme, Mr Field, though he never again knapped full-time, filled in on occasion for Herbert Edwards between the two World Wars.

His father, Robert Field, died in 1915 aged 45. "When I started I sat at my grandfather's block in the family knapping shop at the *Coach and Horses* in Thetford Road. I only knapped. Father quartered and flaked. It's in flaking where the money lies. A bad flaker wastes flint. A good one gets every possible flake out of each core he sits on his knee. Father paid me 1s. 3d. (6½p.) a thousand for my gunflints. It was good money then."

"Our working day began at 7 a.m., but we had breaks for breakfast, dinner and tea, and seldom finished before 8 p.m. There was no flint work on

Mondays. Then I did gardening. On Saturdays we knapped only for the first hour. After that, there was 'telling out'—counting the flints knapped during the week. Father followed the old system. Seating himself in front of trays loaded with flints, he tipped them out in casts of five into tins by his legs, and totted up flints faster than anyone else I ever saw."

Nearly every knapper had within easy reach of his block a series of tins arranged systematically to hold flints of different sorts. The order at the *Coach and Horses* normally ran Single Pistol, Horse Pistol, Large Gun, Chalks and Greys, First Carbines (double backs), Second Carbines (single backs), First Muskets and Second Muskets. The lion's share of this enterprise went to West Africa, but one consignment of flints knapped by the Fields for that market disappeared into a watery grave. It went down with a ship torpedoed by a German U-boat.

"I liked an open-air life so much better," Mr Field said, "for knapping was dull work as well as dusty. You couldn't avoid arm ache as you used the same muscles all the time. Cuts didn't bother me, but now and again bits of flint flew into my face or lodged in an eye."

Allegiance to the craft brought fearful losses to the Field family. Of eight men in one workshop, as W. G. Clarke recorded in *Norfolk and Suffolk* (1921), seven men died in early manhood. A father and three sons all succumbed within four years. Eight widows, the relicts of flint knappers, had a common surname.

Yet, as Mr Herbert Field said, "My grandfather, who was also Robert Field, lived until 62 and was one of the longest-lived full-time knappers on record. His whole life was spent working flint. Some masters grew older but as they aged, they gave more time to business, less to chipping flint."

The fate of women bereaved by the craft's insidious dust is frequently overlooked. How did they cope? Poor relief was minimal. Several had children, sometimes a string of little ones. About the only outlet for spare-time labour in a town serviced by family or owner-occupier shopkeepers centred on its rabbit felting factories, two in London Road and a third in George Street. These provided "homework", doling out rabbit skins in "turns" (sixty skins to a turn) from which the long hairs had to be plucked as these wouldn't felt. Some women after queueing up at a factory door accepted six turns as a week's homework, and earned 1s. 3d. (6½p.) a turn.

In 1907, seventeen knappers and five stone diggers provided the man-power for Brandon's industry. Gunflints, as knapped in one shop, were categorised as Long Dane 1¾ × 1 inch; Fowling 1 3/8 inch square; Carbine 1¼ × 1 inch; Musket 1 3/8 × 1¾ inch; Horse Pistol 1 inch square; Single 7/8 inch square; and Pocket Pistol 5/8 × ½ inch. Long Dane guns, which were manufactured mainly in Denmark and derived the first part of their name from their long barrels, sold readily to Arabs in the Middle East, but also found a big market in Africa. Flints designated Singles fitted single-barrel sporting guns which Birmingham manufactured for its African and Chinese markets.

The First World War threatened to extinguish the industry. Soon after its outbreak knappers of military age joined up and older men went into local armament and engineering factories. But surprisingly a market for strike-a-lights survived. Fred Edwards, as his son told me, shut up his flintworks, stacked almost to the roof with barrels of flints already knapped, and with two horses and a tumbril hired himself to a local haulage contractor.

Yet the old skills were not lost. With the signing of the 1919 Peace Treaty, restrictions governing the movement of arms and ammunition were relaxed, and the industry's seemingly irrepressible spark again flew upwards as tropical markets opened up afresh in West Africa and the Malay Peninsula. In 1924, there were seven knappers in regular employment and two stone diggers, a decade later one knapper fewer and but one full-time stone digger, that veteran and unwearied mole, Arthur Ashley, whose 71st birthday fell in April, 1934.

Earlier, Brandon's trade in strike-a-lights had touched a sensitive political nerve in China. After setting up a useful market behind the Great Wall, this speciality all at once struck a prohibitive barrier because the Chinese authorities took the view that these harmless fire-lighting flints encouraged banditry and banned their import. Whatever sales talk the Chinese merchant put over, some of his customers had formed the habit of picking flints out of their tinder boxes, screwing them into the cocks of ancient flintlocks, and so, happily equipped, sallying forth on a robber's spree.

In 1935 that genial essayist, versifier and lover of cricket, E. V. Lucas, took a look at Brandon. Commenting on its ancient craft in *A Wanderer's Notebook*, his weekly column in *The Sunday Times*, he stirred some readers to recall their memories of flintlocks in the bush.

J. D. McCormick, of Kirkcaldy, Scotland, recalled a regular trade in gunflints in West Africa where Long Danes were the only guns permitted for native use. A Birmingham firm, he supposed, exported both guns and flints. These antiquated weapons blazed off riotously at junketings, especially ceremonies marking the funeral of a "big man", when black powder and whoopee mixed with alarming fire and frenzy. Such orgies, with Long Danes to the fore, he believed, still characterised funeral rites on the Niger Delta.

A former district officer on the Gold Coast, C. H. P. Lamond, who then lived in retirement at Cockfield in Suffolk, had signed hundreds of forms in triplicate licensing chiefs to use "flintlocks known as Dane guns"; he also issued permits for powder and lead. In his experience, the natives though careful to reserve some powder and shot for celebrations, expended much of their firepower in hunting game. He told of one hair-raising sequel. A native stood trial for manslaughter at a Cape Coast Assizes because of his negligence in handling a Dane gun. Asked to tell the court what happened, he explained: "I was on my farm with my gun. The bush moved, and I fired at what I thought was a monkey. Then I found that I had killed my brother."

When I first visited Brandon in 1933, I never dreamed that one day I would settle there; my sole intention was to talk to a flint knapper. Behind *The Eagle* in a stone building housing the Edwards's flintworks, I found "Piper" Field (there was also a "Musket" Field) turning out about 2,000 gunflints a day from flakes he had already prepared; his output earned him 5s. (25p.) a thousand. One flint, he told me, gave sparks for about fifty shots, and a proper flake, as he defined it, was six inches long with a double back. His own family, he reckoned, had been flintmakers for more than 200 years.

At this time the firm of Edwards, father and son, were the industry's major producers and mainstay. In 1934/35, despite a shortage of knappers, they exported more than 800,000 gunflints to China and West Africa. Lagos traded in Horse Pistols, Carbines went to Kumassi, Ashanti and Calabar, and Muskets to Bangkok. All at once the Abyssinian market opened up. In the autumn of 1935, from 35,000 to 40,000 flints a week of different sorts were supplied for the Abyssinian Army. Many of its poorly equipped units had no better arms than flintlocks with which to defy Mussolini's soldiers with their modern weapons and poison gas canisters.

Imitation Stone Age weapons manufactured by William Spalding at Brandon.

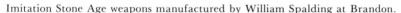

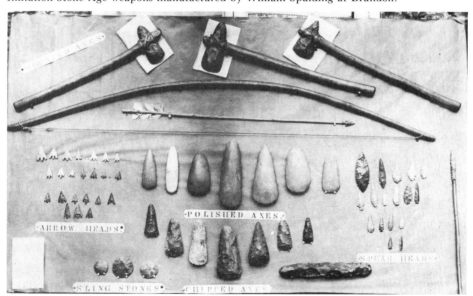

As a change from hammering out gunflints, "Piper" Field knapped "hearts" for church decoration. A fine specimen, chipped out of a solid block, weighed about 5lb; on another which he showed me he had engraved his name. Latterly as a hobby he manufactured arrow heads for archery clubs and exhibits for curio collectors and museum curators.

The Edwards then kept a small private museum. Its relics, which would be highly valuable by today's standards, included muskets, horse pistols and a mail coach guard's blunderbuss as well as an unbroken deer antler pick from Grime's Graves. I also noticed leaf and tanged arrow heads, round sling stones, polished and rough-cut axes associated with Neolithic East Anglia, but one could not tell whether those articles were genuine or examples of current skills.

During his visit to what he erroneously described as a Norfolk industry, E. V. Lucas bought a Brandon-fashioned arrow head, a clever imitation of a Neolithic point. "I shall bury it in the ground where archaeologists dig," he wrote ". . . and why its barbs never had to be torn away from any ancient Briton's flesh only I and the Norfolk knapper know."

Several Brandon knappers crowned their craftsmanship by designing novelties out of flint. In the 1920's Robert W. "Bill" Basham of Town Street attained pastmaster status by chipping a flint necklace out of solid pieces of grey-brown flint. His seventeen hollow circlets or bangles terminated in a heart pendant suspended from a C-shaped flint. Basham claimed his achievement as unique, the result of a process of which he alone had the secret. He needed money badly, so in 1927 he sold his necklace to Sir Mark Collet, of

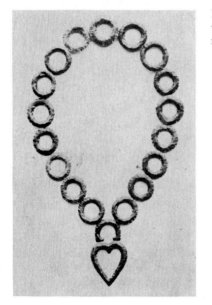

Robert W. Basham's necklace of seventeen circlets which he sold in 1927 for £10. He claimed to have made it by a process of which he alone held the secret.
James English collection

110

William Spalding, left, with a hafted flint axe he had made, Fred Snare, middle, and Arthur Ashley with his pick. *Herbert Field collection*

St Clere, Kemsing, Kent, for £10, although judging by the hours spent on it, he felt it was worth £30. He joined the circlets together with their tailpiece and pendant by lead clips, but it deserved, he thought, what he could not afford, gold links. Sir Mark might have been tempted to supply them before presenting the necklace to his daughter.

The necklace passed into the ownership of Brigadier Hugh Norman, D.S.O., who in 1967 loaned it, along with Basham's correspondence, to the Maidstone Museum. Mr de Lotbiniere saw it there and through the owner's courtesy obtained the loan of it for Brandon's festival in June, 1974. Locals then saw an exquisitely delicate example of flint craft such as no Neolithic chief or adolescent ever draped round a shapely neck. The necklace, worth anyone's admiration, is now on permanent loan at Moyses Hall Museum, Bury St Edmunds.

Every piece of it is fastidiously pressure flaked. To obtain a circle, Basham first struck a core almost dead centre and from the flake containing the resultant bulb of percussion punched out or extracted this bruised spot. He then enlarged this hole and painstakingly flaked in almost microscopic chips the flint's outer edges to get a narrow circlet.

He improved even on this extraordinary example of craftsmanship by cutting the alphabet out of flint discs, each letter about double the size of an ordinary postage stamp. It is difficult to say whether the C, G, K and Q with their squiggles tested his ingenuity more than the A, B, P and R with their tiny apertures; every letter called for sensitive flaking. It occupied his spare time almost unrelievedly for two years to complete the twenty-six letters. His alphabet left Brandon even more mysteriously than his necklace had done. If rumours were believed, an American had bought it, but if a consensus view be accepted, it remains in England, preserved somewhere in Oxfordshire. If marketed, it would probably realise four figures.

Basham, so surgically adroit as a craftsman, died of silicosis in 1932 at the age of 38, his last days passed wretchedly as he lay in bed gasping for air and trying to keep warm, with brown paper pressed against his chest.

In his prime Fred Snare, who was Basham's uncle, demonstrated uncommon dexterity in knapping brittle materials. As Sydney Rogerson noted

Left: The brothers Basham at work, Tom, left, flaking and Bill, the master craftsman, knapping.
James English collection

Opposite: Bill Basham's alphabet, each letter about double postage stamp size. This masterpiece of twentieth-century flint craft represents two years of spare-time labour.
Moyses Hall Museum,
Bury St Edmunds

in 1927, he cut out replicas of antiquity's weapons in crystal, obsidian and glass, his specialities extending to arrow heads chipped out of the thick brown glass of Bovril bottles. Snare studied weapons used by tribal hunters in Polynesia and North America and, if challenged, could imitate very fairly the arrow heads Red Indians once knapped for shooting salmon as well as examples of arrows shafted and shot by Neolithic men hunting deer in eastern England. As early as 1905, he carved a necklace of ten bangles out of solid flint, but not one circlet had the finesse that distinguished Basham's masterly ornament, though he may have inspired his nephew to transcend his technique.

Some sixty Snares lie buried in Brandon's churchyard. As the last scion of that craft dynasty, Fred "Budget" Snare (1858-1934) died with an international reputation as a gunflint expert as well as a leading exporter. Had he held out a month or two longer, he would have celebrated his golden wedding. His widow, Hannah Maria, lived to 95, surviving him by nineteen years. At one stage the Snares employed seventeen men, and she herself turned out hundreds of small bags in which flints, 200 of one sort to a bag, were packed before being crated, frequently in old cocoa boxes, for export. She could also knap competently.

It was her husband's ancestor, John Snare, whose tenacity and common-

Jack Carter with quartering hammer upraised and "Champ" Palmer flaking, with members of the Carter family in the background. *Seymour de Lotbiniere collection*

sense kept the industry alive after the Gunflint Company's collapse. A fine fillip to his determination was the 11,000,000 Carbines ordered by the Turkish Government. However, the traditional richness of this family's association with gunflints is exemplified by a story which, if apocryphal, has the ring of truth to it. When H.M.S. *Victory* was refitted before being placed on public exhibition at Portsmouth, the Snares were asked to supply gunflints for sea muskets and other small arms such as her crew fired at Trafalgar. As Fred Snare commented "That was no trouble. We looked up our work books 120 years earlier, and repeated the order."

Clearly, with flint so subservient to their hammer strokes, craftsmen sometimes baffled archaeologists and museum staffs by their spin-offs or, more exactly, knap-offs. Brandon never bred an imitator of Stone Age weapons and tools with the skill and commercial acumen of Edward Simpson, widely known as "Flint Jack" and also called "Bones". Sydney Skertchly befriended him and learned some of his tricks, but like many others was deceived by his uncannily convincing forgeries. He loved to tell of their meeting in London when the

Flint mosaics manufactured at Carter's flintworks and now preserved at Brandon's Community Centre. *Seymour de Lotbiniere collection*

"untamable, irreclaimable vagabond" said he was determined to go to his grave an honest man. In that hope, he had given up his flint work and was then occupied making Egyptian antiquities for the trade.

A decade earlier "Flint Jack's" fellow northerner, William Smith, alias "Skin and Grief" or "Snake Willy", ran a prehistoric weapons factory on the east coast of Yorkshire. This nest of counterfeits and forgeries formed what the Royal Institution in its transactions, February, 1865, described as "a manufactory of stone hammer-heads, Ancient British urns and flint weapons of all descriptions . . . not only arrow heads and celts of all sizes but rings, knives, saws and even fish hooks of flint were produced, some of which have been engraved as genuine in local archaeological publications." A slippery flint-smith indeed.

Brandon's most accomplished performer in this imitative craft, William Spalding, or "Billy Nummer" as he was called, earned his livelihood as a brick and tile maker at Weeting. Though never a knapper, he employed his spare time to turn himself into a Stone Age implement and weapon fabricator and

115

within a few years gained repute beyond East Anglia for his skilfully made axe, spear and arrow heads, scrapers, knives and sickles, hafted as appropriate. He sold much of his work, sometimes profitably.

Neolithic workmanship challenges the finest modern skills. It is perhaps not so difficult to get near to it with steel-headed hammers. However Mr John Lord, the present warden of Grime's Graves, achieves astonishing imitations by using only knapping tools of the kind available 4,000 years ago, stone, pieces of bone, bits of antler and so forth. With such materials he knaps axe and arrow heads, scrapers and knives, all soundly finished, but his best work in my view is a sickle. In shape and serrations, it assuredly qualifies as a fit exhibit of twentieth century flint craft for any museum in the country. Not a particle of steel touched it.

To revert to the industry's most serious side, its health hazard. Shortly before and in between the two world wars doctors tried to introduce devices that would protect knappers' lungs from flint dust. Dr S.H. Long, founder in 1926 of the Norfolk Naturalists' Trust, interested himself in the problem, and was concerned about the sickness and mortality suffered. He either designed or supplied two specially constructed respirators for men exposed to an unhealthy atmosphere at Fisons' fertiliser works at Two Mile Bottom, near Thetford. About the same time, he arrived in Brandon with another pair, which were tried out by Fred Edwards and his son Herbert. The masks of aluminium had cotton filter pads, and like most masks then patented tended to inhibit breathing. But after sitting and working for a spell in a mask, the knapper had only to unscrew the cap to see how much dust its pad had collected—usually a thick deposit. Despite this salutary warning, most men disliked using the masks. They felt hampered as workers. And accustomed to sitting in hot, ill-ventilated sheds, they complained of feeling abnormally cold, becoming chilled as soon as they took off their masks and went outside. The rapid change in body temperature then experienced worsened their bronchitis, some thought.

Once when he gave a flint knapping demonstration in Norwich Herbert Edwards took from his box of hammers, flakes and flints a beautiful piece of black "floorstone" and showed it to a surgeon working at Norwich Hospital. Dr Long pointed out its keen edge. "It's sharp enough for an operation," he remarked. The surgeon, an extroverted, plain-speaking consultant, retorted: "How do you think they performed operations in the Stone Age?"

CHAPTER TEN

Is this the Industry's Final Phase?

IF PREDICTIONS of its early demise be gathered together, the industry should have died many times during the last hundred years. But in defiance of Jeremiahs, especially those who forecast its end within a decade or so of their scrutiny, Brandon's gunflint industry survived. Prophecy is confounded.

After the Second World War, the industry perked up largely through the initiative and fidelity to it of Herbert Edwards. In 1950, he employed five men in his flint works behind the *Flint Knappers*, of which he was landlord. One of them was Mr Albert "Smoker" Palmer who as a soldier in the Far East had been wounded and held prisoner by the Japanese for three and a half years. Born in March, 1903, he started knapping in his 44th year. When I last saw him in November, 1979, his energy belied his years and his wartime privations.

"After getting demobbed," he said, "I needed a job, and Mr Edwards was short of knappers, so I thought I'd give it a try. It worked all right. Mr Edwards treated me well. He paid me a weekly wage, not a piecework rate, and handed out a good bonus at Christmas. I stuck it for seven years, knapping all the time—I never tried to flake—but I could see the red light. Whatever precautions are taken, and we had dust extractor hoods fixed above our blocks, you can't keep dust out of your lungs."

So, by a chronological somersault, Mr Palmer jumped from the historic past to the prehistoric present, becoming an assistant to the custodian at Grime's Graves.

The insidious dust also worried Herbert Edwards. In a further attempt to counter it, he replaced the hoods positioned over his knapping blocks by vacuum extraction ducts, electrically operated as the hoods had been, but of greater power to suck up particles. They also made more noise, and some knappers preferred not to switch on. In the early 1950's, his five employees averaged about 40,000 gunflints a week, most of which were shipped to African markets.

In 1951, a cousin of his, V. R. "Vic" Edwards, a capable knapper in his day, who was then landlord of the *Coach and Horses* in Thetford Road, reminded me of the unflagging pace he and his fellow craftsmen had kept up forty years ago when their piecework rate was 1s. 2d. (6p.) a thousand for gunflints. "You had to knock out about 3,000 flints a day," he said, "which meant not falling below 250 to 300 an hour if you wanted a living. Today the pace isn't so hot." His markets had not folded up. Even in 1951 he reckoned that he could have resumed his craft with an immediate order of two million gunflints for West Africa. But he did not have the will to do so. Besides, it was a quieter life, and possibly more remunerative, running a pub.

Since stone-digging operations at Lingheath had ceased before the war, the Edwards' enterprise now relied for its flints on quarries widely dispersed in East Anglia. Many tons, brought by truck, were dug out of pits at Whitlingham, east of Norwich, but Herbert Edwards thought their quality never measured up to Lingheath's best. He did, however, get some excellent black flint from a quarry near Sudbury. And one day in 1961, I found him enthusing about 37 tons of black flint he had bought from the Forestry Commission, all of it mechanically excavated from the Widow's Pit at West Tofts, less than a mile north of Grime's Graves.

"It is first-class flint," he said. "If I had to pay a miner to work for me today, his wages would be £10 a week; and to pay that for a ton and a half of black flint would make it impossible for me to continue my knapping business."

In a letter dated 3rd April, 1961, he recorded his craft's output as 42,000 gunflints a month, made up of 32,000 carbine and 10,000 musket flints. At the same time face and random flints were prepared for the building trade, and several tons sent monthly to different parts of Britain.

In the 1950s Lagos was the principal African market for his exports. But by May, 1963, that outlet appeared to be jeopardised by political develop-

"Piper" Field, left, quartering and Herbert Edwards, flint master, weighing out some gunflints.
James English collection

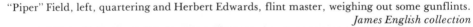

ments in Ghana which if widely adopted meant the end in black Africa of long-established arms restrictions. Instead of being licensed to use only antique guns, its people would be free to fire whatever guns they could afford. "Exports to Nigeria have dropped lately," he said. "In the first three months this year, I sent no more than 50,000 gunflints there. But the outlook isn't too bad, as new markets have opened up in America which took about half that quantity of flints in the first quarter."

The vogue for muzzle loading musketry clubs in the United States might well have stemmed from American airmen who had served at East Anglian air bases in the Second World War, especially at Lakenheath. What cannot be ignored is that in their off-duty hours many hundreds of American airmen flocked into Brandon, saw the flintlocks displayed on the walls of the *Flint Knappers*, and talked to a man at the bar deeply versed in the industry's lore. The West, they knew, had been conquered largely by flintlocks. The more interested ferreted out details about gunflint making; its techniques contrasted refreshingly with their preoccupations about multiple cannon power and the bomb loads carried and dropped by their Flying Fortresses. And, back home again on discharge or leave, they had little difficulty in regenerating this interest, a sequel to which was the life membership conferred by the muzzle loaders of Portsmouth, Ohio, an organisation 4,500 strong, on Herbert Edwards.

More than a hundred units belong today to the Brigade of the American Revolution, their object being to perpetuate traditional weapons and uniforms associated with that bitter struggle. Nostalgia of a similar kind animates Canadians who provide the manpower for recreative units based on the country's museums and historic forts. Old Fort Erie, Ontario, for example, still unfinished after its third rebuilding when war broke out with the United States in 1812, was held alternately by British and American regiments until its last defenders, American troops, blew it up on 5th November, 1814, and crossed the river to Buffalo, so signalising the last presence of U.S. forces on Canadian soil. Now reconstituted and controlled by the Niagara Parks Commission, the fort is very much a tourist attraction. Students dressed in the uniform of British infantry soldiers of about 1812 demonstrate foot and arms drill, including the platoon exercise for loading and firing muskets, and also serve and fire a muzzle-loading cannon of the period. By a roundabout route the flints used in these ceremonial displays hail from Brandon, which strikes the fort's manager, Mr T. J. Shaughnessy, as ironic since "our site abounds with flint and was a prime reason for the Indian settlements situated around here, but the flint, though workable, doesn't compare in quality with the English flint."*

For musketry enthusiasts at home, the parent organisation, the Muzzle Loaders' Association of Great Britain, now has a big fixture list of annual

---

*Gunflints discarded by troops or Indians lie in or around many historic North American forts. During excavations 1959-66, no fewer than 2,536 were recovered at Fort Michilimackinac on Mackinac Island, Michigan, a stronghold on the revolutionary frontier, 1715-81. Of these, 2,182 specimens were wedge-shaped. Of the remainder, not one revealed a technique identifiable with the English (Brandon) mode of manufacture.

competitions, with specific flintlock classes for rifle, musket, pistol and shotgun. Starting in 1972, when the first international matches were held in Europe, the sport has grown to the point at which such a tournament in 1980 drew teams from sixteen nations, women shooters included, and all meetings put up targets for flint matches.

It might be said that trans-Atlantic goodwill or "the special relationship" was cemented in September, 1979, when the M.L.A.G.B. at its "Wimbledon" Championship meeting staged the first full-scale competition between teams representing Britain and the United States. Seventeen separate events were held, the very first of these international shoot-offs being the "Brandon Flintlock Single Barrel Pistol" match, a tribute from both sides of the Atlantic to the town's eminence as a gunflint manufactory. National rifle events, including flintlock rifle and musket competitions, are always shot at Bisley during the August Bank Holiday weekend. There is keen interest also in the National Clay Pigeon Flintlock Team Trophy, a yearly event, in which competitors are allowed two missfires, no more. The "birds" take off, and if a flintlock jams or misses fire, there is no pulling them back.

Back to the Edwards manufactory. In 1967, its proprietor clashed with the Board of Trade because of an order received from a dealer in South Africa. Under the Board's regulations musket flints were classified as arms and embargoed for export to Africa except under licence. "Extenuating circumstances" might be considered, it was said, for issuing a licence. But, whatever these were, they did not extend to long-standing exports of gunflints by the Edwards family to five continents nor to an order lately met for a consignment to Czechosolovakia, an Iron Curtain market opened up by former members of the RAF's No. 311 (Czech) Bomber Squadron stationed at East Wretham, near Thetford, during the Second World War.

Whenever orders for gunflints slackened off, the Edwards works was kept busy cutting facing flints into squares or circles or preparing random flints for precasting by builders into panels to form readily emplaced walling material, a change, too, from uncharismatic brick. No less than 80 tons of flint trimmed in the *Flint Knappers* yard constitute the facade, sectionalised in panels, of the new City Library at Norwich, its grey face catching glints of sunlight in contrast to the nearby Scandinavian-style brickwork of the City Hall.

Church work, too, is undying. A ton and a half of flint helped restore much of the medieval grace of Fakenham's fourteenth-century church of St Peter and St Paul with its imposing west tower, one of Norfolk's finest. Other flints, hammered out from flaking cores, helped to renovate a Trust House property at Winchester. A more unusual order originated from Windsor Castle, where flint flakes of a special kind were required for "galletting", referred to by some architects as "garretting" or even "garrettening", to repair parts of the castle's walls damaged by decay and souvenir hunters. "We had to save," a knapper told me, "those flakes first cut from a 'quarter', showing 'chalk heel' — a strip of white rind."

The exceptional longevity enjoyed by Herbert Edwards and Fred Snare must not obscure the craft's inescapable hazards. James Waterman knapped on his own for two years in a yard behind the *Coach and Horses*, but died aged 48 in 1948 from a form of silicosis. Arthur "Trixie" Drewry, a most efficient all-round post-war knapper, an Edwards employee, died early from thrombosis, but not before teaching the craft to his son-in-law, Mr Fred Avery.

Fred Avery, left, and his father-in-law, Arthur ''Trixie'' Drewry, preparing building flints in the yard of the *Flint Knappers.*

What Edwards enjoyed besides longevity was the international prominence his craft earned. It brought him letters and requests for gunflints specimens, even nodules of the famous black flint, from all parts of the world, and collectors of flintlocks sought his advice on difficulties met with in firing their ancient pieces. In translating letters for him, mainly from France, I recall a collector from Charente who complained of having " 'des ennuis' avec la mise à feu de mon pistolet á silex, marque Grosvin Liege." His trouble lay, he felt, either with the poor quality of his flint or the poor shape he'd given it. Another collector, writing from Marne, needed two flints to fit a French infantry rifle of the 1777 model, one flint for a cavalry mousqueton of the First Empire, and two flints for a hunting gun manufactured by Monsieur Jalabert Lamotte of Saint Etienne, Loire, "modele du chien de fusil de chasse."

Samples of gunflints Edwards was then selling and photographs of his knappers at work, their hammers and raw materials, were sent to Meusnes,

Loire et Cher, where Monsieur Jean Emy established what he proudly styled the only gunflint museum in existence.* As the author, too, of France's most comprehensive work on the subject, *Histoire de la Pierre à Fusil*, M. Emy devoted chapters to such topics as the origin of flint, secrets of its manufacture, precarious life of the *caillouteurs*, illnesses and accidents associated with the craft, exports of gunflints, contraband traffic in flints, and so forth. In his view Meusnes, for more than three centuries, was "le centre mondial" for the production and cutting of pierres à feu.

Without belittling his claims and eschewing if possible a local prejudice, I would transfer that distinction for 150 years at least to Brandon. In its favour, an arbiter must give weight to the industry's greater activity since Napoleon's defeat, and its accessibility to East Anglia's rich, far from exhausted bed of silky black flint, a stimulant and indeed an inspiration to knapping skills since early times.

An incident not to be forgotten of Commonwealth affection for the Crown linked to a historic relic occurred in 1952 when a New Zealander, Mrs Galbraith, presented the Queen with a pistol once owned by Flora Macdonald and, in all probability, handled by Bonnie Prince Charlie. It would be fitting, she felt, if it could be passed at a later date to the Duke of Cornwall, the future Prince Charles, who was then a small boy.

Hearing of this, Herbert Edwards prepared two cases of gunflints, one filled entirely with pistol size, but each flint a hand-picked specimen of the kind still being knapped. He sent these to the Superintendent of Works at Windsor Castle, in the hope that, if found acceptable, they might accompany the pistol. To his intense pleasure, he received a letter dated 28th November, 1952, from Buckingham Palace under the signature of the Assistant Private Secretary, Sir Martin (now Lord) Charteris, acknowledging the gift "of the two beautiful presentation cases of flints" and concluding "I have laid these before The Queen, and Her Majesty has commanded me to thank you very much indeed for this delightful present which she is pleased to accept on the Duke of Cornwall's behalf."

Not only did Herbert Edwards maintain the industry and cherish his family documents and historical records relating to its pursuit until the end of his life, but he had the reputation of being a good employer. When the standard local wage was about £10 a week, he paid his knappers £14 or so, and kept them happy at Christmas. His last address, Lagos Palm, Bury Road, Brandon, was a reminder of his most lucrative trading centre. Such a house name, however incongruous its appearance in a Suffolk road, raised a gleam in the eyes of knowing passers-by.

At his death in 1973 his son-in-law, Mr James English, took over the business and continued it in the Edwards name. Under his management, it meets requests for gunflints, building flints and ornamental flints from

---

*In July 1980 M. Emy transferred his gunflint museum from Meusnes to Lucay le Male.

whatever source they arise. He has supplied gunflints to muzzle loaders in lands and cities as geographically disparate as Fiji, Hawaii, Williamsburg and Montreal. Enthusiasts have flown in, making personal visits, from West Germany, Italy, Austria and Australia. In 1975, he completed an order for the United States that would have troubled the ghost of George III. Colonel Vincent J. Keyhoe, Commanding Officer of the 10th Regiment of Foot at

Herbert Edwards with two cases of gunflints presented to the Queen to accompany a flint-lock pistol that had belonged to Flora Macdonald, the pro-tectress of Bonnie Prince Charlie.
James English collection

Chelmsford, Massachusetts, asked for a collection of gunflints for display during his regiment's bicentenary celebrations of the Declaration of Independence, 1776.

In 1980, Mr English and one part-time knapper, Mr Fred Avery, held the fort. The latter quarters, flakes and knaps and has an output ranging from 70,000 to 75,000 gunflints a year, a part of which goes to hobbyist flintlock organisations in the United States.

He knaps four sorts, Musket 1 1/8 inch square; Rifle 3/4 inch square; Horse Pistol 5/8 inch square and Pocket Pistols 3/8 inch square. Like yesterday's craftsmen, he never uses calipers or any kind of measure when hammering out gunflints;he knapped the tiny double backed pocket pistol flint, shown in the illustration, in semi-darkness. But he uses a template when the job consists of working to an architect's designs specifying ornamental flints of a particular pattern for church porches, buttresses, clerestory parapets, inscriptions, friezes and so forth. In 1979 he cut out shapes to repair gaps in flintwork panels at Felsham Church, Suffolk, and in March, 1980, Mr English showed me designs required for flint replacements at St Andrew's Church, Walberswick; he also had flints to cut for St Mary's, Kersey, the church on the hill overlooking Suffolk's most photographed village.

Quartering hammers, as used in the Edwards shop off Rattlers Road, weigh 3 to 3½ lb in weight. "It must have a soft head," he says. "Hard steel won't do. The best flaking heads are knocked out of old bits of railway line.

Mr James English at his knapping block in Rattlers Road, Brandon.
James English collection

When you get a new hammer from the blacksmith's, its face is smooth; you must rough the point a bit before it bites. And it will soon need pulling out. If I flaked full time for a week, I'd need a new hammer at the end of it, or the points of the old one pulled out. Once worn, they won't flake well, and each point, to start with, shouldn't be more than one-eighth inch square."

After picking up the craft from his father-in-law — he started when 20 as a full-time knapper in the Edwards flintworks in 1953 — Mr Avery once succeeded in knapping 400 gunflints in an hour. A fast worker at all times, a man, too, who enjoys work, he has struck as many as 200 flakes off one "quarter", and from a single flake of best quality black flint knapped six gunflints.

Having split thousands of nodules in his time, in their insides he opened up fossils of cockle shells, sea urchins and squid bones. Round nodules, about half football size, often contain an inner nodule which like the outer one is covered by a hard white rind. But set in its solid flint, Mr Avery finds things that remind him of Kent's Cavern, Torquay—spicules resembling a miniaturised cluster of stalactites, but not frozen!

"As I now work by myself," he said, "I find it quicker to strike small flakes and make just one gunflint out of each flake. When you hold your flake flat face uppermost against the stake and cut it, the part you're not holding may slide down your apron into a tub or container. Then when you've trimmed the flint in your hand, you lose time picking up the flake's other part from chips below."

The craftsman, whose precise timing and sureness of touch coalesce into swift-flowing, rhythmical movements, first trims the back or heel, then the sides of his flint, still held flat face uppermost against the level-headed stake, each blow falling on its nearside, an eighth of an inch away. He then turns the flint over and undercuts the firing edge.

Some knappers trimmed their flints all the way round and never bothered about the turnover or reverse cut. This did not please any master who spotted it. Nor did he look unresponsively at a pile of nodules exposed to frost or heaped too near a shop's fire, well aware that flint, when ice cold or overheated, becomes "crazed", its texture breaking up into tiny crackles.

In this inflationary age, it is not surprising that the price of gunflints per thousand has rocketed, as much as £40 a thousand being a recent rate for piecework. But to earn it, the knapper must quarter and flake his flints before he can knap.

As to the black powder shooter's price overseas, this is too variable to specify a sum, but I have heard of Americans paying 75 cents for each Brandon-knapped gunflint. If it furnishes their muskets or pistols with sparks enough for fifty or even twenty-five discharges, it is but a modest outlay in the total cost of their atavistic, romantically evocative, history soaked, explosive hobby.

We are left with a question posterity alone can answer. On the face of it, the craft appears close to its final curtain in Brandon. There is not a young knapper in sight today. But who dare venture a forecast that flint as a stone for man's shaping has arrived at the end of its phenomenal service line?

When the stone diggers and knappers of axe heads, knives, scrapers, borers, microliths, sickles and arrow heads deserted Grime's Graves about 1500 BC, not one could have known or guessed that ahead lay entirely new ages of flint craft.

125

Select Bibliography

Archer, H. G. The Oldest Industry in England, *Wide World Magazine* pp. 527-533, 1906.

Baggallay, Frank. The Use of Flint in Building, especially in the County of Suffolk. *Transactions R.I.B.A.* new series, Vol. 1, 1885.

Backmann, John. *A History of Invention and Discoveries,* translated from the German by William Johnston, Third Edition, Vol. III, London, 1817.

Blackmore, Howard L. *British Military Firearms, 1650-1850,* London, 1961. *Guns and Rifles of the World,* London, 1965.

Bosquett, Abraham. *The Young Man of Honour's Vade Mecum,* London, 1817.

Boston, Noel. *Old Guns and Pistols,* London, 1958.

Brown, David. Firesteels and Pursemounts Again, *Bonner Jahrbucher des Rheinischen Landesmuseums in Bonn,* 1977.

Cautley, H. Munro. *Suffolk Churches and their Treasures,* London, 1937.

Clark, J. G. D. *Prehistoric Europe,* London, 1952.

Clarke, Rainbird. The Flint-Knapping Industry of Brandon, *Antiquity,* Vol. IX, pp. 38-56, 1935.

Clarke, W. G. *Norfolk and Suffolk,* London, 1921.

Christy, M. The Bryant and May Museum of Firemaking Appliances, Catalogue of Exhibits, 1926.

de Lotbiniere, Seymour. The Story of the English Gunflint: Some Theories and Queries, *Journal of the Arms and Armour Society,* June, 1977. English Gunflint Making in the Seventeenth and Eighteenth Centuries. *The Minnesota Archaeologist,* Vol. 39, No. 2, 1980.

Dunham, Keith. *The Gun Trade of Birmingham,* Birmingham, 1955.

Emy, Jean. *Histoire de la Pierre à Fusil,* Selles sur Cher, France.

Evans, John. *The Ancient Stone Implements, Weapons and Ornaments of Great Britain,* London, 1872.

Forrest, A. J. *Under Three Crowns, craftsmen in flint,* pp. 21-27, Ipswich, 1961.

George, J. N. *English Guns and Rifles,* Plantersville, South Carolina, 1947.

Graham, P. Anderson. *All the Year with Nature,* knapping flints, pp. 53-68, London, 1893.

Harrison, J. Park. *On the British Flint-Workers at Brandon,* Report of the British Association for the Advancement of Science, pp. 626-27, 1880.

Harvey, John. *Medieval Craftsmen,* London, 1975.

Hawker, P. *Instructions to Young Sportsmen,* London, 1814.

James, Dr M. R. *Suffolk and Norfolk,* London, 1930.

Johnson, Walter. *Folk-Memory,* Oxford, 1908.

Lenk, Torsten. *The Flintlock; Its Origin and Development,* translated by G. A. Urquart and edited by J. F. Hayward, London, 1965.

Lovett, Edward. Gun Flint Manufactory at Brandon, *Proceedings of the Society of Antiquarians of Scotland,* pp. 206-212, 1886/7.

Margary, Ivan D. *Roman Roads in Britain,* London, 1955.

Martin, Thomas. *The Circle of the Mechanical Arts,* London, 1813.

Oakley, Kenneth P. *Man the Tool-Maker,* Sixth Edition, British Museum, 1972.

Olson, Alison Gilbert. *The Radical Duke, Career and Correspondence of Charles Lennox, Third Duke of Richmond,* OUP, 1961.

126

Peacock, A. J. *Bread and Blood; A Study in the Agrarian Riots in East Anglia,* London, 1965.

Prehistoric Society of East Anglia, Report on the Excavations at Grime's Graves, Weeting, Norfolk, March-May 1914.

Prehistoric Society, *Proceedings* for 1918-19.

Public Record Office, Board of Ordnance documents held at Kew. Of particular value is class WO 47 containing "Journals of Proceedings" (1644-1696 with gaps) and Board Minutes.

Rann, Ernest H. A Pre-History Factory, chapter in *Bygone Suffolk,* edited by Cuming Walters, London, 1902.

Rogerson, Sydney. The Oldest Industry in the World, *Blackwood's Magazine,* pp. 525-534, 1927.

Royal Institution, On the Forgery of Antiquities, *Transactions,* February, 1865.

Salzman, L. F. *Buildings in England Down to 1540,* OUP, 1967.

Scott, W. H. *British Field Sports,* 2nd edition, 1820.

Shepherd, Walter. *Flint,* London, 1972.

Sieveking, G de G et al. A New Survey of Grime's Graves, Norfolk. *Proceedings of the Prehistoric Society,* Vol. 39, 1973.

Skertchly, Sydney B. J. On the Manufacture of Gun-Flints, *Memoir of Geological Survey of England and Wales,* 1879. Glacial Man: My Part in his Discovery, from *Proceedings of the Royal Society of Queensland,* Vol. 33, 1921. *Catalogue of the Skertchly collection,* compiled by himself, in Queensland Museum, Fortitude Valley.

Suffolk Churches. *A Pocket Guide,* Suffolk Historic Churches Trust, Woodbridge, 1976.

Suffolk Record Office. Parish registers and records for Brandon along with Letter Books of Brandon Gunflint Company and miscellaneous documents relating to the town's flint knapping industry.

Tennyson, Julian. *Suffolk Scene,* London and Glasgow, 1939.

Victoria History of the Counties of England: Suffolk, Vols. I & II, London, 1911.

Watson, William. *Flint Implements,* British Museum, Third edition revised by G. de G. Sieveking, 1967.

Wyatt, James. On the Manufacture of Gun Flints, pp. 578-590 in *Flint Chips* edited by Edward T. Stevens, London, 1870.

Musket, rifle, horse pistol and pocket pistol flints knapped by Mr Fred Avery in 1980.

Index

Illustrations in bold type.

Brickyard workers, 26
Bridewell Museum — *See* Norwich
Brighthampton, firesteel, **40**
British Association for the Advancement of Science, 87
British Museum, 2, 8, 25, 34, 41 F/N
Brown, David, 40
Brown Besses, 52, 120
Brownlee, James, 78
Brunswick, Julius, Duke of, 46
Bryant & May Museum, catalogue of, 41
Buccaneers, 77
Burgh Castle, 39
Burgon, John, 55, 74, 80
Burke, Edmund, 53
Burres, Charles, 60
Bury Free Press, 7
Bury St Edmunds, 55, 59, 67, 69, 102, 111
Butley Priory, 43

C
Cadogan, Lord, 56
Caillouteurs, 51, 53, 63, **64,** 97, 122
Caistor-by-Norwich, 40
Calabar, 109
Calivers, 45
Calyon, 44
Canada, 52, 99, 100, 123; ceremonials, 119
Carbines, 48, 51, 103
Cannon, 50, 119
Carriers, flint carters, 71, 72
Carter, William "Billy", 12
 — William, 78
Catton, 91
Cerne Abbas, Dorset, 1
Chalk goddess, 33
Champagne, France, 51
Charity Commissioners, 15
Charles II, King, 48
Charles Edward, "Bonnie Prince Charlie", 122
Charteris, Sir Martin, 122
Chelmsford, Mass., 123
China, 98, 108, 109
Christy, M., 41
Churches, 42, 43, 44, 66, 68, 69, 102, 105, 106, 120, 124
Cissbury Ring, Sussex, 29, 37, 38
Civil War, 47
Clarendon, 62
Clark, A. J., 34

Clark, Lord, 43
Clark, Robert, 78
 — William, 59, 62
 — William, Jnr, 59
Clarke, Roy Rainbird, 98, 99
Claxton, James, 78
Coach & Horses (public house), Brandon, 106, 107, 117, 121
Cockfield, Suffolk, 108
Collet, Sir Mark, 110, 111
Colossus, H.M.S., 101
Common rights, 13
Const, Frederick, 60
Cook, Richard, 79
Copenhagen, National Museum, 94
Cornwall, Duke of, 122
Couffy, France, 64
C.P.R.E., 7
Cretaceous Age, 1
Crimean War, 43
Croydon, Surrey, 97
Croxton, Norfolk, 57
Culford, Suffolk, 6
Curry, R., 62
Curson, William, 84
Curzon, Josiah, 62, 78

D
Daggers, flint, **26, 93,** 94
Darwin, Charles, 94
de Lotbiniere, Brig-Gen. Joly, 99
 — Seymour, 55, 56, 89-91, 99-102, 111
Deer, red stags, 31, 35 — *See* also antlers
Devil's Hollows, 30
"Dockey" 104
 — bag, 19
Dolomieu, Citizen, 64, 89
Domesday Book, 41
Dongworth, Thomas, 62
Dorchester, 2, 100
Douro, schooner, 101
Dover, chalk cliffs, 1
Dowsers, British Society of, 8
Dunwich (Donewich), 44
Dyaks, Borneo, 94
Dyer, Frank, 18
 — Helen, 67
 — Jack, 18
Drewry, Arthur "Trixie" (1904-66), **x,** 121

INDEX

E

Eagle, (public house), Brandon, 3, 11, 109
East Anglia, Univ. of, 41
East Anglian Daily Times, 7, 8
Eastern Daily Press, 7
East India Company, 76, 78
Easton Down, Wilts, 29, 37
East Wretham, 120
Edwards, Frederick, 8, **10,** 116
—Herbert (1892-1973), 8, 9, **10,** 11, 12, 18, 19, 21, 22, 106, 116, 117, **118,** 119, 121, 122, **123**
—Victor Robert (1898-1963), **86,** 117
Emy, Jean, 121 F/N, 122
Enclosure Award 1810, 13
English, James, 122, **124**
Environment, Dept. of, 38
Elizabeth II, Queen, 122
Ely Abbey, 41
Ewell, Thomas & Sons, 80, 82

F

Fakenham, Norfolk, 120
Felsham, Suffolk, 124
Feltwell, Norfolk, 15
Field, Herbert, 106, 107
—Robert (1869-1915), **9,** 106
—Robert (1848-1910), 107
—Herbert "Piper" (1877-1939), 12, 109, **118**
—James, 87
Field Sports, 68
Fiji, 123
Firesteels and Pursemounts Again, 40
Firesteels, 40, 41
Fish-hooks, flint, **95,** 115
Fitch, Canon John, 42
Flaking, 10, 76, 92, 96, 106, 124
Flakes, **75**
Flaked core, **90**
Flint Chips, 91
Flintcraft, 8-11, 94, **95,** 96, 97, 116, 125; Church bldg, 44; Cottage, **12;** Facing stones, 92; French, 51, 63-65; German learners, 51; Imitations, 109; Mosaics, **115;** Novelties, 110-113; 'Platform' construction, 90; Wall bldg, 105, 106; Turkish, 82
"Flint Jack"—*See* Simpson, Edward
Flint Merchants, Dutch, 51
Floorstone, 18, 19, 22, **25,** 32, 33, 56, 57, 85, 89, 93, 96, 97, 100

Forestry Commission, 6, 7, 13, 118
Forsyth, Rev. Alexander John, 74
Fort Michilimackinac, 119 F/N
Foulden, Norfolk, 15
Fowling-pieces, 46
Fox & Hounds (public house), Brandon, 87
Foxes, silver, 16
Francis, Edward, 78
Frewer, emigré, 91
"Friction Lights", 75
Fruer, French POW, 65
Fusil Boucanier, 77

G

"Garretting", 120
Geological Society, 95
—Survey, 94
George III, King, 123
Germany, 47
German artificers, 51
Ghana, 119
Gipping, Suffolk, 43
Gislingham, Suffolk, 44
Glossary of East Anglia, 21 F/N
"God Dolly", Somerset, 34
Goering, Herman, 35
Gold Coast, 108, 109
Good Hope, Cape of, 84
—Castle of, 51
Goodwood, Sussex, 56
Graham, P. Anderson, 88
Great Massingham, 29
Greenhithe, 61
Greenland, sealers, 84
Greenwell, Canon William, 30, 31, 35
Greenwich, 48
Grief, A., 62
—Elizabeth, 58, 59
Grime's Graves, 2, 7, 8, 18, 21, 23, 56, 97, 99, 100, 116-118, 125; Exploitation, 29-38; Floorstone, **25;** Goddess, **33;** Neolithic pit reconstructed, **28;** Picks—*See* Antlers; View of, **6;** Visitors, 34 F/N
Guinea Coast, 77
Gunflints, 5, 8-11, 53, 55, 56, 68, 69, 74, **75,** 76, 83-85, 89, 124; Barrels for export, **70;** Counting and recording, 83, 84; Diagram of, **65;** Museum, 121 F/N; Prices for, 58, 62, 63, 79-81, 89, 92, 103, 104, 109, 117; Sorts, 54, 57, 61-64, 84, 95, 96, 107, 123
Gunmakers, 57

INDEX